Publishing & Printing Terminology for Self-Publishers

A Seriously Useful Author's Guide

Jane Rowland

t

Copyright © 2010 Jane Rowland and Troubador Publishing Ltd

The moral right of the author has been asserted.

Apart from any fair dealing for the purposes of research or private study, or criticism or review, as permitted under the Copyright, Designs and Patents Act 1988, this publication may only be reproduced, stored or transmitted, in any form or by any means, with the prior permission in writing of the publishers, or in the case of reprographic reproduction in accordance with the terms of licences issued by the Copyright Licensing Agency. Enquiries concerning reproduction outside those terms should be sent to the publishers.

Troubador Publishing Ltd
5 Weir Road
Kibworth Beauchamp
Leics LE8 0LQ, UK
Tel: 0116 2792299
Email: books@troubador.co.uk
Web: www.troubador.co.uk

9781848761698

A Cataloguing-in-Publication (CIP) catalogue record for this book is available from the British Library.

Typeset in 11pt Baskerville by Troubador Publishing Ltd, Leics, UK

Printed in Great Britain by the MPG Books Group, Bodmin and King's Lynn

Publishing & Printing Terminology
for Self-Publishers

Contents

Acknowledgments

I would like to thank all at Troubador Publishing—especially Julia Fuller and Jeremy Thompson—for their contribution to this book.

Introduction

Self-publishing has become increasingly common as authors continue to struggle to land that elusive publishing deal. Advances in technology and changes within the books retail industry have helped to reduce the cost, and fuelled the ease, with which self-published books can be published and sold.

There are now numerous ways of 'publishing' a book—from websites where you upload your own text and cover files and pay to have them printed, through to bespoke services offered by skilled publishing companies. The choice may look bewildering at first, but it really all boils down to what you want. If you simply want a few copies of your book printed for family and friends, then go for a cheaper option—if you want to see your book on the shelves of a high street retailer, then you will need proper industry insight and a high quality product to sell.

Despite all the advances in technology, many self-publishers still find getting to grips with the whole industry to be a steep learning curve. The publishing industry has various technicalities and vagaries of book design and manufacture, and there is the often arcane and impenetrable books distribution and retail trade to overcome when you actually have your book in your hand.

As a self-publisher you will usually encounter publishing and book trade terminology that you will need to know and understand. Clarity is the key to successful self-publishing—and this book has been specifically written to help you obtain that clarity when dealing with printers, self-publishing service providers and the retail trade.

Publishing and Printing Terminology for Self-Publishers grew out of a two part article first published in the *The Self-Publishing Magazine* in 2008. The response to these articles was amazing—with our readers requesting ever more words and phrases to help them understand some of the complexities of the publishing world and books trade. This book is an expanded version of those original magazine articles, which we hope will assist any self-publisher to make the right choices for them.

This is not simply a glossary, however; it is also crammed full of fantastically useful information which makes it essential reading (from A–Z... literally!) for all self-publishers.

The Self-Publishing Magazine—the UK's only print based magazine dedicated to the subject—has a reputation for offering great advice to all self-publishers—we sincerely hope you find this book continues that tradition.

Happy reading!

Jane Rowland

Editor, *The Self Publishing Magazine*

www.selfpublishingmagazine.co.uk

How to use this Book

This book has been produced to help you get the most from your self-publishing project. We recognise that everyone will have slightly different reasons for self-publishing, and that they will be going about the process in a slightly different manner. Therefore, the guide has been written to cover the phrases you *may* encounter, regardless of how you approach self-publishing.

The glossary section is laid out alphabetically—which means that it will be quick and easy for you to find the words you are looking for. You can use the glossary 'on demand' to search out the words you need, then and there. However, it will also be invaluable for anyone embarking on the self-publishing process to consider reading the entire glossary. This will give you a much better overview of the entire self-publishing process.

The style of the glossary has been kept as simple as possible —so you should be able to quickly locate the words you need and also swiftly check out related entries.

To give you an overview of how to get the most from the

glossary, we have given a described example below—with a brief description of how to 'read' each entry.

KINDLE

The E-BOOK READER designed and sold by AMAZON. It is now available in the United States and the UK. The Kindle is unique as an e-book reader (at the moment) in that you can download books wirelessly from Amazon. Most other e-book readers currently require a physical computer connection.

The Kindle can read several E-BOOK formats, including MOBIPOCKET and EPUB, but the main format (designed for it) is AWZ.

The **bold** type is the main entry—we can see that this entry is about the Kindle. Any text in SMALL CAPS indicates words/phrases/terms which are also defined and discussed elsewhere within the glossary, and which are related to the main entry shown in **bold**. So if we look up E-BOOK READER (which we can locate either by looking it up in the main text alphabetically, or by looking in the index), we can learn more about E-BOOKS and how they relate to the **Kindle**—the first word we looked up.

At the end of the book there is an index, which will allow you to quickly check the location of a definition/explanation of a particular word, and every other occasion that that word is mentioned in the glossary.

Note that when touching upon subjects—such as contracts and copyright—that have some legal bearing, we give only a very basic overview. We strongly recommend that you seek legal assistance should you have any more specific queries, rather than relying on the broad information outlined in this book.

To simplify the glossary further, we have made the following two definitions, which reflect how we differentiate between self-publishing and mainstream/traditional publishing:

> *Self-publishing* is defined as an author-funded publication, where the author is responsible for all of the publishing costs. We do not differentiate between self-publishing in the truest sense (ie. doing everything yourself) or using a self-publishing services provider.

> *Traditional publishing* or *mainstream publishing* is defined as the opposite of self-publishing. A mainstream or traditional publishing company is responsible for all the costs involved in a project, pays an advance and/or royalties to an author and takes all the financial risk in its publication.

We have endeavoured to cover all of the words, phrases and terms you are likely to encounter, but if we have missed anything that you think should be in the guide, or you have found an entry that you think could be improved, do please let us know so we can update the book in future editions. You can email the publishers at *admin@troubador.co.uk* to leave feedback.

We have also made a web page available, where we shall be post definitions of words that readers have suggested post-publication. You can view this page here:

www.troubador.co.uk/general/PTTupdate.pdf

Glossary

A

ADVANCE

(Strictly, an 'advance against royalties received from sales')

A payment made to an author either on the acquisition of a MANUSCRIPT or upon delivery of the manuscript to a publisher. The author's ROYALTIES from book sales must earn back the advance paid; only then will an author start to receive any further royalties. Advances are only applicable to MAINSTREAM PUBLISHING; a SELF-PUBLISHING SERVICES PROVIDER is not going to pay the author an advance (and it would be questionable if they did as the author is funding the publication). Advances are based on the PRINT RUN and the projected sales of a book. Thus, new authors are unlikely to receive large advances.

ADVANCE COPIES

You may be asked to provide copies of your book in advance of publication, for booksellers or WHOLESALERS to look at when making buying decisions, or so that you can get ENDORSEMENTS from well connected and influential people for your book before the full PRINT RUN. In cases where the book has not yet been printed, you would need to provide the MANUSCRIPT either as a print out or as an electronic file (you can mark this type of proof 'Uncorrected, unbound proof'. If the book is printed, you can supply an actual copy. Some authors print a small number of copies in advance, and clearly mark the copies as 'advance copies' or 'uncorrected proofs'. These copies are then sent for review or for advance endorsement. The benefit of doing this is that it allows you to use any forthcoming endorsement or review on the cover of the final book, rather than have to wait to add any endorsements to a future edition. However, it will be more costly to print copies in advance, as effectively you are then arranging two print runs. You also have to be firm and set deadlines for receiving reviews or endorsements, otherwise you'll be waiting forever before you get your final book to print. If sending the book for advance endorsement in file format, try to protect your work from illegal copying, and clearly mark the manuscript as a proof copy that asserts your own COPYRIGHT.

ADVANCE INFORMATION (AI)

An Advance Information sheet is used to announce a title to the books trade. An AI should be on a single sheet of A4 paper and contain key information about the forthcoming title, including: Title, author, publishing imprint, a brief synopsis, author biog, price, PUBLICATION DATE, ordering information, ISBN, the book jacket image (if available), and the classification (see BIC CLASSIFICATION) of the book. You can also add information about the marketing of the book, especially if you have got advertising or press coverage organised. Your AI needs to be emailed or mailed to the WHOLESALERS, BOOK BUYERS at the chain bookshops, LIBRARY SUPPLIERS and independent stores. If you are targeting your local bookshops, make sure you stress you are a local author—you may find having a local and a national version of the AI useful for targeting each area effectively. The books trade likes to have information on new titles as far in advance of publication (up to 20 weeks) as possible. Before sending out your AI, ensure that your BIBLIOGRAPHIC DATA has been submitted to the relevant agencies, as the recipients of your AI may well look up your book on the BIBLIOGRAPHIC DATABASES—it will look unprofessional if the title is not listed. Remember also that an AI is a selling tool—resist the temptation to go into great detail about the book's content, this is not the place.

ADVERTISING

Advertising is defined as any form of persuasive, paid for communication. Advertising can be a hit and miss affair for self-publishers, and getting 'free' content (articles, features, reviews) may do more for your book's sales than paid-for advertising. If you are going to advertise you have numerous options, such as adverts in magazines and newspapers or online. Large publishers often launch campaigns on buses and on billboards at London Tube stations—but these are likely to be beyond the budget of most self-publishers.

Some top tips for advertising include: if placing an advert in a newspaper or magazine, check the readership is relevant to your work (ask to see the MEDIA PACK or RATE CARD); don't waste money advertising your book in a publication that has no relevance to you or your work. Badly designed adverts can do you a disservice, as can error-filled adverts. If you are not a designer, get the publication to create the artwork for you and PROOF READ it carefully. People often forget to include the most basic information, such as how to order! Don't cram the entire synopsis into the advert, and look for a striking tag line.

Advertising is usually sold by the amount of space an ad occupies (1/4 page, full page, half page, etc.).

Online advertising is charged at a different rate to print-based ads, and you usually pay on a CPM (cost per thousand impressions) basis, and not a flat fee. Targeted advertising will work best for your book, don't use a scatter-gun approach. You may be able to get a newspaper to take a free 'advert' for your book in exchange for some copies that you donate for a 'competition', so be creative when thinking up your approach to advertising.

When placing an advert, ask for the rate card, and then negotiate money off (few publications sell their advertising space at the official 'rate' advertised on the rate card). As a general rule, the closer to the publication date of the newspaper or magazine, the larger the discount you can get off the given advertising rates.

Don't place one or two ads and then sit back and wait for the orders to come pouring in. If you do use advertising, consider it to be one of your awareness-raising tools, not the only tool!

In MARKETING, repetition is the key to making sales, and often consumers have to identify with a product many times (7+) before they will decide to buy.

You should be sent a copy of the advert in the relevant publication, with an invoice, once published.

AGE BANDING

The age band is a guide to the reading age that a publisher believes the book is most suited to. Age bands are starting to be introduced on the back cover of children's books, and are designed to be used by parents, family members and educators to help select books. Age banding has been denounced by some children's authors and library organisations, because they fear that it will discourage readers from buying books. It is not a requirement to give a reading age on a book.

AMAZON

The world's leading Internet bookseller, which has websites in many countries, including North America (Amazon.com), the UK (Amazon.co.uk), Canada (Amazon.ca) and Japan (Amazon.jp). Not content with being a leading book retailer, Amazon have recently moved into publishing, and have also launched an EBOOK READER (known as the KINDLE).

If your book has a UK ISBN, it will appear on the Amazon.co.uk website (whether you want it to or not). The book will usually be sourced by them from UK WHOLESALERS such as GARDNERS or BERTRAM BOOKS when ordered, unless you are in the AMAZON ADVANTAGE.. They also have other schemes that may be useful for self-publishers, such as AMAZON MARKETPLACE and AMAZON LOOK INSIDE.

While many self-publishers have a love/hate relationship with Amazon, they are the largest UK INTERNET RETAILER, so you stand to lose sales if your book is not easily available on their website. If you want your book to appear on Amazon.com (and therefore be available to order in the United States), you may need to investigate using a DIGITAL PRINTING service that, for a price, can make your book available from within North America. Non UK Amazon sites rarely order UK books direct from the UK because the international shipping costs involved make it far too expensive (and TERRITORIAL RIGHTS can prevent such sales).

AMAZON ADVANTAGE

The Advantage scheme ensures your book will be held in stock at the Amazon.co.uk warehouse and dispatched the next day (or even the same day) when ordered by a customer. However, to join the scheme you have to agree to Amazon taking 60% of your cover price. This makes the Advantage scheme uneconomic for many self-publishers (especially if you are using DIGITAL PRINTING to print your book, as the UNIT COST can often mean you will be selling at a loss). If you are not in the Amazon Advantage scheme, your book will usually be listed on their website as 'hard to find', and there may also be an additional 'finder's fee' of £1.99, which the customer must pay, and a default delivery time of 4–6 weeks. This often deters customers from ordering your book. One way around this is to sign up as an AMAZON MARKETPLACE seller. If you supply Amazon on their Advantage scheme, you must also supply your books on CONSIGNMENT.

AMAZON LOOK INSIDE

By uploading the content of your book to the Amazon Look Inside program as a PDF file, customers on the Amazon website are able to 'look inside' your book—view the contents and read a couple of pages—before they choose to buy it, much as they would in a normal bookshop. You have to join the scheme (currently free) before you can send files to the Look Inside program. Authors often worry about COPYRIGHT issues, and potential readers being able to read the whole of their book online, or print pages off, but only limited parts of any book are made available to a browser. A restricted number of pages can be viewed at any one time, and the contents cannot be downloaded. See also GOOGLE BOOK SEARCH.

AMAZON MARKETPLACE

Amazon have a 'marketplace' on their website, where anyone can list books they wish to sell. When someone is looking to buy a book, they can either buy it new from AMAZON, or they can look at the 'New and used' options listed alongside, and, if they so wish, buy it from another seller who is offering the same book via the Amazon website. If you want to sell your books on Amazon but don't want to give the large discount associated with the AMAZON ADVANTAGE scheme, you can list your book on Amazon's Marketplace at a price you are happy with. When you make a sale via Marketplace, Amazon will take the money from a customer and pass it on to you (less their fee, which is based on a small percentage of the sale price), so you do not need to be able to accept credit card payments from customers yourself. Authors often offer signed copies and speedy delivery to entice Amazon customers to order from them, rather than direct from Amazon or through another Marketplace seller.

AUDIO BOOKS

These are books produced in audio format. Historically these took the form of CDs or cassettes, but today MP3 audio files are an increasingly popular format for audio books. Publishers can sell the audio rights to a book (see RIGHTS). With the advent of online services such as iTunes, audio books seem to be becoming more popular, as it is now possible to download audio books for MP3 players such as iPods from online stores. It is possible to self-publish audio books, but remember that, as with printed books, it pays to get professionals involved to get the best quality project—and for unknown authors they can be hard to market (and distribute). Creating an audio book involves recording an actor reading your book, adding music and special effects where relevant, and as such it is a process best left to professionals with the necessary studio facilities, otherwise it can be a very costly process.

AUTHONOMY

A website launched by HarperCollins, where authors can

upload some of their work and other users can read it, rate it and give feedback. Any highly-rated work will, it is promised, be brought to the attention of HarperCollins editors who regularly use the site to look for new writing talent. In 2009, Authonomy issued their first contracts for works discovered via the website—though of the three contracts placed, one manuscript was already being represented by an agent, and another had already been successfully self-published and had a sales track record.

AUTHOR QUESTIONNAIRE

Your publisher, SELF-PUBLISHING SERVICES PROVIDER, marketing service or publicist may ask you to fill out an author questionnaire. This is a detailed form, all about your book and you as its author, which will enable the people working for you on your book to see what the book is about, and what you can bring to the marketing of it. The information provided on this form is often used as the basis for the book's web page, back cover BLURB and all MARKETING activities, so if you are asked to fill one in it pays to fill it in properly.

AVAILABILITY STATUS CODE

These codes inform the books trade about the availability of your book (and are used by BIBLIOGRAPHIC DATABASES, DISTRIBUTORS, WHOLESALERS and publishers). They are usually displayed as abbreviations, such as IP (In Print), NYP (Not Yet Printed), OOP (Out of Print) and TOS (Temporarily Out of Stock). The availability status codes will be disseminated via NIELSEN BOOKDATA and similar bibliographic databases to shops and wholesalers.

If you are in charge of your own BIBLIOGRAPHIC DATA it pays to update it in a timely fashion, informing the main agencies of any changes in your book's availability, as incorrect listings will adversely affect your sales.

AZW

An e-book format linked to the KINDLE ebook reader. See E-BOOKS, E-BOOK READERS.

B

BACKLIST

A backlist is all of the titles previously published by a publishing company (or self-publishing author). In a bookshop, the new title displays or the special offers at the front of the store are most generally for FRONTLIST (i.e., new) books. The rest of the shelves (usually towards the back of a store, and organised alphabetically) are given over to backlist (older) titles.

It can be harder to market backlist titles than frontlist, unless (for example) a film of a book is coming out and a publisher can remarket the title based on that. New titles tend to become backlist titles after a period of 6-12 months—less for books printed in HARDBACK format.

Frontlist and backlist as concepts will have less importance for most self-publishers—after all, you will often be marketing your 'new' book over a longer period time than a mainstream publisher (who will have more pre-publication MARKETING). The frontlist/backlist concept is useful for you to understand when approaching bookshops with a book that was self-published some months ago. As with many things, retailers are always more interested in what is new than what has been available elsewhere for some time.

BACKORDER

See DUES

BARCODE

If you wish to sell your book through the major retailers and WHOLESALERS, you are going to need to have a barcode on the book cover. Barcodes are used throughout the SUPPLY CHAIN to ensure accuracy of distribution. Barcodes also allow retailers to keep track of stock and sales of titles (which happens when the barcode is scanned at the cash till, see EPOS). If you are not using a SELF-PUBLISHING SERVICES PROVIDER (who will usually supply or assist with barcodes) then you will need to generate your own. There are lots of free internet sites where you can turn your ISBN into a barcode, which can then be placed on your book (for most paperbacks this will be on the back cover, for HARDBACKS it will be the back cover or inside flap of the DUST JACKET). To avoid problems with barcode scanning you need to ensure you do not make the barcode too small. For more information about barcodes, and the industry standards for their usage, see *www.bic.org.uk*

BERTRAM BOOKS

A leading book WHOLESALER, serving both chain and independent bookshops. To ensure your book is as widely available as possible, you will need to approach Bertram Books and look at opening an account with them. They have a very helpful website, which contains useful information for new publishers. If your distribution is being handled by your SELF-PUBLISHING SERVICES PROVIDER, or printer, ensure they have an account with Bertram Books. Many bookshops, including the independents, have accounts with Bertram Books and use their Bertline system to check stock and place orders. Bertram Books also produce newlsetters and magazines for their retail customers, which pick new titles and list pre-publication offers and special deals on new books. See also WHOLESALERS and WHOLESALER CATALOGUES

BDS

BDS run the BRITISH LIBRARY CATALOGUING-IN-PUBLICATION PROGRAM (CIP). Importantly, they also collate and disseminate BIBLIOGRAPHIC DATA to libraries throughout the UK—so if you can submit your bibliographic data to them early enough, it will then be sent out to all participating libraries. BDS have useful information, and a data submission sheet, on their website. *www.bibliographicdata.com*

BIBLIOGRAPHIC DATA

The data specific to your book's ISBN that is submitted to bibliographic databases and then disseminated to the books trade. The data shows the title, author, subject classification, availability and ordering information for the book. Book industry standards suggest that the bibliographic data for a book should be disseminated to the books trade up to 22 weeks in advance of its publication. See also NIELSEN BOOKDATA, BOWKER, BDS.

BIBLIOGRAPHIC DATABASES

Bibliographic databases are up-to-date repositories of

information about all in print (and recently out of print) books. NIELSEN BOOKDATA hold the main UK bibliographic database. Shops, WHOLESALERS and libraries pay for a subscription to these databases to allow them to look up a title and place orders. The databases contain all the key information about a book, and are driven by the ISBN. Nielsen BookData holds the largest bibliographic database in the UK, but others exist, such as those kept by BOWKER and BDS.

BIC CLASSIFICATION

The BIC Standard Subject Categories & Qualifiers scheme is the most commonly used book classification scheme. It defines how books are organised, by subject area. This system standardises the classification process. Each publisher (and this should include you) will use codes to help booksellers and libraries classify books into subjects. If you are in charge of your own ISBN, then you'll need to specify a BIC code when you send details of your book to NIELSEN BOOKDATA (and other bibliographic databases). It also makes sense to use it on your ADVANCE INFORMATION (and anything else you use to market to the books trade). You can search for the right classification for your book here: *http://193.128.166.228:3000/*. Guidance about how to pick the right codes for your book can be found on the BIC website: *www.bic.org.uk*

BINDING

Paperbacks are produced with perfect, limp, notch or burst binding. This is the method used to fix the pages onto the SPINE and cover using glue. The edges of the pages may also be notched to retain more glue, making the binding more durable. Sewn binding is also glued, but individual sections (usually of 16- or 32-pages) are then sewn with thin twine into the spine, then glued, making it stronger. Stitching is often used when a book is very long (+400 pages), because without sewn binding it may be too heavy and fall apart. Books with only a few pages could be SADDLE-STITCHED (i.e., stapled), in which case there is no spine at all.

HARDBACK books are case bound. Two pieces of card (front and back covers) and a spine are covered in cloth, and often BLOCKING (usually lettering in silver or gold FOIL) is then stamped onto the spine and/or front cover. Around that a DUST JACKET is wrapped, folding around the hard cover. The BOOK BLOCK (the book's text) is then stuck to the inside of the hard case cover using END PAPERS, which are either plain (unprinted) or printed.

Some hardback books (eg. children's, cookery, etc.) may have a hardcover but no dust jacket wrapped around. A printed cover is stuck onto the hard case permanently, and this is known as a PPC (printed paper case) cover.

BITMAPPED
There are several definitions of bitmapped, but the one you will most likely encounter is when the scanned resolution of a picture is insufficient for it to be printed without distorting, leading to a image which shows as individual pixels rather than a whole image. This is sometimes also called pixelated.

Printers working on your files may tell you that graphics are low RESOLUTION, and warn you that they will print as bitmapped or pixelated. Pictures supplied for print need to be at least 300DPI (DOTS PER INCH) in resolution, at the size at which they are to be printed, to print correctly (i.e., without bitmapping).

BLAD

(Short for Book Layout And Design)

A pre-publication sales and MARKETING tool used by mainstream publishers for FRONTLIST books. Often, blads consist of a small stapled booklet containing a sample chapter and showing the book's layout and style. For self-publishing authors, there are more cost-effective marketing materials available, such as posters and leaflets, which can be produced as part of a marketing push. A blad will not necessarily get the best results at the most efficient cost in terms of marketing a single title.

BLEACH

Bleach is used to whiten paper pulp and thus make paper whiter. All paper goes through a form of bleaching. Recycled paper requires more chemical bleaching than newly made paper, thus making it less environmentally friendly. The whiter the paper, the more bleach has been used in the paper-making process. See also FSC and PAPER.

BLEED

Used to describe an illustration, image or text that will exceed (i.e., go beyond) the page dimensions. When a page is trimmed to the book's finished size, the image will 'bleed' off the edge of the paper. Using a bleed has a cost implication when printing, because you have to take account of the extra wastage needed to trim off the bled image (it can cost more for a book to have images/text that go right off the edge of the page as a result). Bleeds are common in design work, and most book covers have a bleed. Books can look more stylish if images bleed off the edge of the trimmed page, but you will need to ask printers to quote 'with a bleed' because of the potential cost implications.

BLOCKING

This is the text that has been 'stamped' onto the cloth-covered hard case of a HARDBACK. Usually the blocking is done in a coloured FOIL (silver and gold are common), stamped onto the SPINE of the book (nearly always) and possibly the front cover as well (which adds to the cost of production). Just as you should be able to choose the colour and texture of the cloth covering of your cased book, you should also be able to choose the foil colour. Slip off the DUST JACKET of a hardback title and the majority will have foil blocked letters on the spine, and some on the front too. It is possible to use EMBOSSING on the hard case as well, rather than or in addition to foil, should you prefer. See also BINDING.

BLOG (BLOGGING, BLOGGERS)

Blogging has become an online social networking phenomenon—anyone can become a blogger, all they really need is access to a computer. There are people blogging on every conceivable subject, including books. Some book bloggers have a huge following and a large readership, and they review any books that take their fancy—including self-published books. They can start a fantastic word-of-mouth buzz about a book. Many self-publishing authors are becoming bloggers—starting their own blogs about their writing, books and life in general. The most successful bloggers are active online, posting regularly and getting involved in other people's blogs.

To get the most out of a blog you have to be regular, genuine and active. Some book bloggers specialise in talking about books they love, some review books and others blog on a whole variety of topics, which includes books, publishing, self-publishing and marketing. Some bloggers have thousands of followers—people who read and comment about the blogs—others have only a few. Many have seen the rise of blogging as the ultimate in self-publishing—you can 'publish' your thoughts to the world at large via the internet. See SOCIAL NETWORKING and TWITTER.

BLURB

A short, succinct and pithy description of a book, usually found on the back cover, but possibly on an inside flap of a hardback DUST JACKET. Blurbs are also used in MARKETING and on websites. If you are handling your own ISBN data, when you notify the details of your book to NIELSEN BOOKDATA you'll be asked to supply a short description (less than 350 words) and a long description (any length) for your book. These will be disseminated across the books trade—to Internet booksellers, bookshops and WHOLESALERS, and anyone else who takes a data feed from Nielsen BookData—so do give your blurbs sufficient thought. Don't simply repeat your short description as the long description; not only is it a wasted chance to tell people about your book in more depth, but some online retailers simply reproduce both descriptions on their websites verbatim (depending upon the data feed they use). Instead, write an eye catching short description, and then elaborate, but don't repeat yourself, in the long description. You'll be thankful you spent the time getting this right once the data about your book has been disseminated and appears on the websites of all the leading retailers. If you are using a SELF-PUBLISHING SERVICES PROVIDER and they are putting the information about your book on the BIBLIOGRAPHIC DATA sites, do make sure you happy with what has been supplied.

BOARD

The paper or card that is used for the cover of paperback books. Board varies from 200 GSM up to about 300 GSM in thickness for paperbacks, and up to 2400 mic for the card used in HARDBACK covers. See PAPER.

BOOK BLOCK

This only applies to LITHOGRAPH PRINTED books. Printers sometimes send a 'book block' to the publisher for approval before the books are bound. Book block therefore refers to the text of the book once it has been printed, folded and trimmed, but before it has been bound. Remember, at this stage the books have been printed—they have not printed one copy of the text and trimmed it for you—all of the books you've ordered have been made into book blocks and are waiting to be bound. Don't think of the book block as a proof—if you spot errors at this stage, it will mean that the relevant text will have to be resupplied, reprinted and retrimmed, and that will be expensive... and at your cost. Ensure you have checked your work *before* you receive a book block! If you are using DIGITAL PRINTING then you will not see a book block, because digital presses automatically print, trim and bind the book in one linear process, instead you'll need to order one copy of your digitally printed book to check.

BOOK BUYERS

Book buyers in this context are not the end user (i.e., people who go and buy your book in a bookshop or direct from you). Instead they are the important decision makers in the book chains and WHOLESALERS who choose what will appear on the bookshelves and stock lists of their company. Book buyers work well in advance, so to have any hope of getting picked up, send them your ADVANCE INFORMATION (AI) as early as you can. Most chains have a head book buyer who oversees a team comprised of, say, a fiction buyer, non-fiction buyer, children's buyer, etc. Wholesalers tend to have buyers who deal with specific publishers. Generally, buyers are looking for books that will sell. Most wholesale buyers are happy to look at self-published books, if they perceive them as having a commercial market. Similarly, chain retailers will support self-published books IF they can see that such titles will earn their shelf space in stores—which can be hard to prove. If your book is not selected as CORE STOCK, then it should still be possible for a reader to order it through a retailer, usually on SPECIAL ORDER, as required. Before approaching book buyers, ensure that you (or your self-publishing services provider) have registered your ISBN and that your BIBLIOGRAPHIC DATA has been submitted correctly. See also BUYING CALENDERS.

BOOK COLLECTORS

Book collectors seek out books that have, or may in the future have, increased value. They look for books that are hard to find or which have a story that makes them collectable. Some self-publishers have unexpectedly found that their books have become collectors' items. For example, Deborah Lawrenson self-published *The Art of Falling*, and as the book grew in popularity, it was picked up by Random House, who gave the author a MAINSTREAM PUBLISHING contract. As soon as this news became known, the self-published edition became a collectable item, with collectors hunting out copies (and paying over the odds to buy them). There are two magazines dedicated to book collecting in the UK which are good sources of further information (see *www.firsts.com* and *www.collectors-club-of-great-britain.co.uk/magazines/default.asp? magazine =12*).

BOOKDATA

See NIELSEN BOOKDATA.

BOOKSELLERS' ASSOCIATION

A trade association for booksellers to which 95% of the UK

and Ireland's booksellers (i.e., bookshops) belong. It exists to consult, lobby and offer advice and support to bookshops. They have some really useful publications, such as a guide listing all their member bookshops by region, which makes it an interesting research tool for self-publishers looking to build links with their local bookshops.

BOOKSURGE

Now part of AMAZON, Booksurge is a DIGITAL PRINTING services provider that also offers online self-publishing. Based in the US, they are mainly US focused, but can be used by UK self-publishers to make a title available from within the US.

BOOKWOVE

A popular paper type, often used to print novels on. Usually either cream or white in colour, and slightly textured. See PAPER.

BOUND

Once a book has been printed, it is bound as specified by the publisher. BINDING refers to the act of the trimmed pages and book covers being fastened together and glued or stitched.

BOWKER

A US-based BIBLIOGRAPHIC DATA agency which has now opened a UK office. They collate bibliographic information on UK titles, which they disseminate, in a variety of ways, to their worldwide bookselling and library customers. You can submit information to them in a number of ways (posting or emailing your ADVANCE INFORMATION sheet, for example, or by using their data template, available from *www.bowker.co.uk*).

BRITISH LIBRARY

The British Library holds the National Book Collection (NBC) —copies of every book published in the UK. As a publisher you have a legal duty to deposit copies of your book (at your cost) within the National Collection. For more information, see LEGAL DEPOSIT and BRITISH LIBRARY'S CIP PROGRAM.

BRITISH LIBRARY'S CATALOGUING-IN-PUBLICATION (CIP) PROGRAM

The Cataloguing-in-Publication (CiP) Program provides information on new and forthcoming books in advance of publication. The scheme is run on contract by a firm called BDS, on behalf of the BRITISH LIBRARY. See BDS.

BROMIDE

See CHROMALIN.

BULK

A printing term, describing the thickness of a book. Also called the depth. The bulk will depend on the number of pages in a book and the type and weight of paper it is printed on.

BURST BINDING

See BINDING.

BUYERS

See BOOK BUYERS.

BUYING CYCLES/CALENDERS

BOOK BUYERS in shops, chains and WHOLESALERS have a buying calender/cycle to which they adhere. When selecting books to stock or promote they work some months in advance. Therefore, when picking books for summer read promotions, they will already have chosen the featured books by early spring, at latest. Buying calenders (sometimes available on request from the major wholesalers and chains) will reflect their deadlines for publishers to submit new title information to them. For example, the deadline for submitting information about a new book that you intend to publish in June 2010 will be around February 2010.

C

CAMERA READY COPY (CRC)

This refers to the book, as supplied to a printer by the publisher, which is ready for printing. The printer expects to make no changes to the files submitted (and if they do, they will charge for the changes they make on top of the agreed price for printing). Today, books are almost always sent to print as electronic files, but historically hard copy was sent and then 'photographed' onto printing plates, hence the term 'camera-ready'. If you lay out your book in a word processing or typesetting program, you will usually be asked to supply PDF files for printing (the simplest way to supply PRINT READY files today). More on this under PDF.

CASE BOUND

See BINDING.

CASED

See BINDING.

CAST OFF

A method used to estimate the final typeset page extent from a MANUSCRIPT. A text file is imported into a template of the correct dimensions in a TYPESETTING programme, and this gives a more accurate estimate of the page EXTENT. This allows for a more accurate quoting on the cost of producing a book. This is relevant if you are asking companies to quote for typesetting your book, or so that you can ask printers for a costing based on a certain page extent.

CENTRALIZED BUYING

With centralized buying, all book buying decisions are made by a retailer centrally, not by local branch managers. Waterstone's, for example, makes CORE STOCK decisions centrally, though branch managers can also make local buying decisions.

CHROMALIN

A high resolution print out supplied by a printer that accurately shows colour reproduction. The printer uses the same COLOUR SEPARATION files to photographically produce a composite so that colour reproduction can be checked.

CLOTH

The fabric covering of HARDBACK books. You can usually specify a cloth colour, and a printer should be able to show you a SWATCHBOOK of the different textures and colours of cloth available.

CMYK

A colour model used for colour printing. With traditional

printing, colour printing is carried out using a four-colour process, printing Cyan, Magenta, Yellow and Black (CMYK) plates to make up all other colours. However, the process is limited in that CMYK cannot reproduce all colour ranges accurately. If a picture that has been supplied as an RGB (Red, Green, Blue) image is printed by a printer on a CMYK press, then strange results can be produced. For this reason, lithographic printers usually ask for all images to be supplied as CMYK graphics. In the LITHOGRAPHIC PRINTING process, paper is passed through four different presses in a line, with each colour added on top of the others. For this reason, colour printing is more expensive than printing only in black. See PROCESS COLOURS, SPOT COLOUR and COLOUR SEPARATION.

COATED PAPER
Paper that has been specially coated to offer strength and reflectivity; often used for books of photographs as they hold ink in a superior way to uncoated papers. See also PAPER.

COLOUR CALIBRATION
It is worth noting that colours display differently on almost everyone's computer screens, due to different colour calibration from the graphics cards and monitors on computers. This means that if you spend a long time tweaking the colour balance of photos and graphics so they look just right on your computer screen (or when you print them on your inkjet printer), the images may look different when output by a different printer or displayed on a different screen. To

work around this, in LITHOGRAPHIC PRINTING, ask to see an output proof of any colour work. You can usually resupply files without incurring large charges if the colours are not what you expect to see. If you are working with DIGITAL PRINTING, you may need to actually order a copy of your book before you are able to check colour work, due to the nature of the printing processes.

COLOUR PLATES

See PLATES.

COLOUR SEPARATION

With traditional (LITHOGRAPHIC PRINTING), colour printing is carried out using the CMYK colour model. To achieve the best results, each of the colours used has to be separated out (into Cyan, Magenta, Yellow and Black) before printing can start. This separation is done using special software and equipment, and you will not (usually) be expected to supply your own colour separated files.

CONSIGNMENT

If you are asked to supply books 'on consignment' you are effectively agreeing to send the customer the books they ordered at your cost and without invoicing them until the books have been sold by that customer. After a set period of time, any sold books are credited to you and the unsold ones will be returned. This is how the AMAZON ADVANTAGE scheme, amongst others, works. If you agree to supply on consignment, you cannot insist on pre-payment.

CONTRACTS

A written contract is a legally binding agreement between you and the company you are engaging to undertake work on your behalf. It will be signed and dated by yourself and a representative of the company you have signed with. In self-publishing, a QUOTE will often form part of the contract, so it is essential to make sure that the quote is correct. Both parties have recourse in law if either side breaks the written contract (called breach of contract).

Not all disputes arise because of disreputable firms; sometimes disputes arise because the self-publishing author did not fully understand the terms of the contract. If you are in any doubt about the services that are on offer, double check *before signing* the contract. A good contract should make explicit the nuts and bolts of the arrangement (i.e., what exactly you get for your money, how the service works, etc.). Issues such as extra fees and ROYALTIES should also be in the contract or accompanying paperwork. You must never be pressured into signing a contract without having had the time to check it over to your satisfaction. Contracts may cover items such as:

- When you are expected to pay for the services you have contracted.
- Who owns the RIGHTS to the work (if you are self-publishing, the rights should remain with you).
- The nuts and bolts of the deal you are signing up to (i.e., some SELF-PUBLISHING SERVICE PROVIDERS and printers will print copies to meet orders, some print all the copies

in one go, etc. Your contract should say exactly what is being done on your behalf.

• What royalty agreement (if any) you have signed up to and how/when royalties will be paid.

Generally, anything you have in writing, if it shows intent, can be legally binding, so if you make changes to the contract, confirm those changes in writing (for example, you may change your mind about the number of copies you want, confirming that change in writing can be a good idea to avoid problems later). Be a little wary if you are offered no written contract. Oral contracts exist, but they are open to interpretation should a dispute occur, because it is harder to prove what was promised verbally (your word against theirs). If you do not have a written contract, try to confirm everything you agree in writing, and keep a dated copy for yourself.

(Note that this entry is a very simple overview of what a contract is—you are advised to take professional advice before signing a contract if you have any doubts.) See also LETTER OF AGREEMENT and TERMS AND CONDITIONS.

COPY EDITING

A process undertaken before a book is prepared for publication (and before TYPESETTING). A MANUSCRIPT will be 'marked up' by a copy editor, who is looking for errors in spelling, grammar and semantics. Copy editors may also comment on anything in a manuscript that is unclear or inaccurate. A copy edit can be conducted onscreen (on a computer) or on the manuscript itself—you can decide which you prefer (onscreen may be a cheaper option, but errors are easier to spot on a printed copy). Historically, copy editors also marked up manuscripts with stylistic and typesetting marks, but nowadays this is not the case so often. It is not a copy editor's job to critique the content a manuscript.

COPYRIGHT

The author's (illustrator's, photographer's, etc.) right to retain ownership of their work—and therefore to profit from their own work. Lasting from 70 years from the end of the year in which an author dies (with exceptions). Copyright is a complex area. Under UK law, an author's work is protected by copyright the moment is is written, and when your book is published it carries a date which proves copyright at that date. The problem can arise in proving copyright to a work, especially when it is unpublished. We suggest taking professional advice for any specific copyright queries you may have. A general overview of copyright law can be found at *www.ipo.gov.uk/types/copy.htm*

CORE STOCK

Core stock represents a book chain's or wholesaler's 'central range'. It is the stock they are most keen on selling, and it is equal to a tiny percentage of the books published in the UK in any year. Core stock is usually chosen by the central BOOK BUYERS— local managers may have little or no say over the space they have to allocate to it. Core stock may also be selected if publishers 'pay' for a spot—in a 3-for-2 offer, bookshop catalogue or prime window display. This is common practice, but book chains tend only to offer such opportunities to books which already fit their core range. See also CENTRALIZED BUYING.

COVER SPREAD
See COVER TEMPLATE.

COVER TEMPLATE
A template or proof that shows the entire cover—front cover, spine and back cover. If you are using a SELF-PUBLISHING SERVICES PROVIDER, who is taking care of your cover design, they are likely to send you a full cover proof for your approval or comment. If you are sending your own files to a printer, you may be able to request a cover template (an empty template) set to the correct dimensions of your book (but this does depend upon the printer/self-publishing service you are using, some don't supply them). If your supplier does not offer a cover template you will need to communicate with them to ensure your template is the right dimensions. If you are having a DUST JACKET, you will need to give extra thought to the SPINE width and wrap around flaps, and may require additional assistance if a template is not supplied for you. Do bear in mind that the width of the SPINE on any cover proof is determined by the page EXTENT and paper weight—so you cannot finalise a cover design until the book is typeset.

CREDIT TERMS
Credit terms vary in the books trade from 30–90 days *in arrears*. Find out the terms before supplying a retailer. If you are supplying on CONSIGNMENT, different terms may apply.

CRITICAL ASSESSMENT

A critical assessment is an in-depth editorial assessment carried out on your work to assess its readability, potential market appeal and, in some cases, its chance of success. You will usually pay for a critical assessment to be carried out on your MANUSCRIPT, and there are many companies who offer to do this. Reputable companies will point out flaws in your work, and not simply offer unchecked praise. Some VANITY PUBLISHERS used to hook potential authors by giving glowing critical assessments indicating potential for great sales, and then offering to publish the work at the author's (great) expense. A good critical assessment should be an honest appraisal of your work, and you need to be able to deal with (and act upon) any criticisms made. Rarely is there nothing that cannot be criticised about an unpublished manuscript, so be prepared to seriously consider negative feedback.

CROP MARKS

The marks on printed or electronic proofs that show where the book will be cropped (trimmed) when printed. If you are having your book typeset, it is recommended that you trim a couple of the pages yourself to the crop marks at the proof stage, so you can see just how the text will look on a page when printed. Are the crop marks too close to the text at either side, top or bottom? Does the text look squashed onto the page once the extra white space has been trimmed off? Proofs will usually be sent to you centred on A4 sheets of paper, but in most cases books will be printed to a different size, so cropping the page down at proof stage can give you a better feel for the way the text will look in the final printed book—and it gives you a chance to check that the MARGINS are set as you wish them to be.

Crop marks will also show you where any elements within your page design will BLEED off the edge of the trimmed page. This may have a cost implication, so make sure you understand whether your book will be printed with or without a bleed.

If you are using a cover template supplied by your chosen self-publishing supplier, then make sure you understand their crop marks so you do not position elements too close to, or too far from, the cropping area.

If you are printing in colour, whether CMYK or SPOT COLOUR, crop marks may also include colour information, including the colour separations or PANTONE colours used in the book. Check these carefully, especially in printer's proofs.

$$D$$

DATA AGGREGATORS

See BIBLIOGRAPHIC DATABASES.

DEPTH

See BULK.

DESK COPY

See ADVANCE COPIES.

DEWEY DECIMAL NUMBERS

A system for classifying books on library shelves. The system has been expanded and updated since its introduction in the 1800s, and it is now used worldwide for library classification.

DIGITAL CONTENT

Publishers continue to seek new ways of generating income from their content. Thus they are digitizing their books and offering the digital content in as many ways as possible. Publishers are also looking at new markets—such as the mobile phone market—as revenue streams for their digital content. For example, some travel publishers have arrangements where travel guides are available to be read and used on mobile phones. Publishing is still finding its way in the digital age, and much of what is being tried by the mainstream is currently experimental—it does not necessarily generate fantastic income. Expect to see increased relevance to self-publishers when it comes to looking at ways of making money out of licensing content over the next few years. See E-BOOKS and DIGITAL RIGHTS MANAGEMENT.

DIGITAL PRINTER

A digital printer is effectively a very large laser printer. The electronic files are fed into the machine and the book is printed using toner, bound and trimmed and a finished book emerges at the end. See DIGITAL PRINTING.

DIGITAL PRINTING

Digital printing was a revolution to the book industry. It allows for very small numbers of books to be printed, cost effectively. The set up costs are minimal, and copies can be 'run off' to order when required. The per copy price remains the same for digitally printed books, with the first copy printed costing the same as the 700th copy. (This is different to LITHOGRAPHIC PRINTING where the per copy price drops the more you print.)

Digital printing is often spoken of synonymously with PRINT ON DEMAND, PoD or 'publish on demand', which is the method of book printing many SELF-PUBLISHING SERVICE PROVIDERS rely on. But digital printing can also be used very cost-effectively for larger print runs. For example, up to 500 copies of a novel can often be printed more cheaply with a digital printer than with a lithographic printer. Mainstream publishers also use digital printing technology to keep books in print and for high value, low demand books.

You need to do your sums carefully if opting to use digital printing, especially if you want to sell through the books trade, as you may find that the large TRADE DISCOUNTS mean that you lose money selling your book once the PER COPY PRICE and shipping has been taken into account. If you want lots of copies printed in advance, or want to take advantage of the economies of scale that printing a larger number of copies brings, it is not cost effective to use digital printing.

DIGITAL RIGHTS
The rights sold to a publisher by an author, which licenses the publisher to use or sell the digital rights of their product. See RIGHTS. Digital rights are often now part of a publishing contract for mainstream authors. Self-publishing authors will need to check whether digital rights are included within any contract taken out with a SELF PUBLISHING SERVICES SUPPLIER.

DIGITAL RIGHTS MANAGEMENT (DRM)
A means of restricting access to a digital file so that it cannot be copied or disseminated to anyone other than the purchaser. The access rights belonging to a user (usually the purchaser of an E-BOOK) allow them to access and use only the digital content to which they are entitled. As publishers seek to make money from DIGITAL CONTENT, they are having to look at

DRM to protect the products they are making available digitally. DRM impacts on such things as how many computers an e-book can be stored upon, how the e-book can be shared etc.

DIRECT SALES

Sales made where no sales discount is applied, so that the full cover price is received from that sale. For a self-publisher, direct sales can help offset the heavy discounts that the retail trade receives, and it can bring the break-even point of a project closer. Self-publishers can make direct sales by encouraging customers to buy from their own website, rather than from INTERNET RETAILERS. They can also make direct sales to family, friends and acquaintances, or by selling copies after speaking engagements, at fetes, and so on.

DISTRIBUTOR

A commercial company that acts on behalf of a publisher to take and fulfil retail (trade) orders. Distributors will handle returns, deal with invoicing and customer queries. In return you pay a percentage of the net sales (or sometimes a flat fee) for using their services. Distributors will hold stock and issue reports relating to the activity they have undertaken on your behalf. Large distributors are unlikely to take on clients who have only a single title, or a very small turnover.

Many SELF-PUBLISHING SERVICES PROVIDERS will act as distributor—for either a percentage of the cover price or a flat fee—for the titles they have helped you to produce.

Alternatively, you can distribute your own book—which means undertaking invoicing, chasing payments, packaging and sending out books that have been ordered, and dealing with any retailer RETURNS. Some WHOLESALERS will sometimes act as a distributor for smaller publishers.

DOUBLE-SPACED

Most mainstream publishers request that submissions are made with type double-spaced. Essentially this involves leaving one line of blank space between each line of text. If you are submitting your MANUSCRIPT to a SELF PUBLISHING SERVICES PROVIDER for COPY EDITING prior to publication, it is a courtesy to present it as double-spaced, to allow the copy editor space to 'mark up' the manuscript. If you are submitting your manuscript for an appraisal, CRITICAL ASSESSMENT or for a QUOTE, it is less important to present it double-spaced.

DPI

Abbreviation for Dots Per Inch, which refers to the resolution of a picture. For print projects you need pictures to be at least 300dpi in resolution at the picture's final size; less than this resolution the printed image will be blurry. Laser printers often print out at 300dpi or 600dpi; LITHOGRAPHIC PRINTING is usually at 2400dpi in resolution. However, images still need to be presented at minimum 300dpi. For web only projects, you need only have images at 96dpi, because computer screens only display at this resolution. See RESOLUTION for more information.

DRYING

Once printed (and this refers to LITHOGRAPHIC PRINTING only), pages will need some drying time. Printers like to leave pages to dry before BINDING: first to avoid smudging of wet ink, but also so that the paper does not dry out too much post-binding and shrink, making the binding too tight.

DUES

If you receive an order for your book before it is actually available, you will often be asked to hold it 'on dues', or on 'backorder'. This means that you are keeping the order ready to fulfil as soon as the book becomes available. It is a courtesy to inform the company who has ordered the book of the status of their order, especially if the publication is delayed. The books trade has some abbreviations that define a book's status, the main ones are: NYP (Not yet Printed), OP or OOP (Out of Print) and TOS (Temporarily Out of Stock), which you may need to use when reporting on a book's status. You are often requested to only hold NYP titles on dues—for books temporarily out of stock or unavailable, you may find that the retailer asks that you do not record any dues as they will reorder when the book is available.

DUST JACKET

A wrap-around jacket that slips over a cased book. The inside flaps are the edges that wrap around the front and back covers to hold the dust jacket on the cased book. The inside flaps are also often used for extra information about the book or author. If you are preparing (or commissioning) the artwork for a dust jacket, bear in mind that you need to get the SPINE width right—if you allow too little space for the spine, the text intended to appear on the spine will be off-centre (which looks unprofessional), and the inside flaps won't have enough reach to wrap around and stay put. Once you know the spine width, a printer should be able to provide you with a template—or at least the dimensions—to help you with the design. Dust jackets can be EMBOSSED, and are usually LAMINATED to prevent tearing. They rarely have printing on the reverse.

E

E-BOOK

An electronic book which can be read only through the use of an electronic reader (e.g., a computer or handheld device). e-books have been around for a while, and have been seen as a way of self-publishing more cheaply as it does not involve actually printing of the book. With the launch of dedicated E-BOOK READERS, many in publishing feel that the time of the e-book has finally arrived.

The e-book drawback at the moment is that many of the newly launched e-book readers use proprietary formats, so you have to decide what FORMAT you are going to release your e-book in. You can release an e-book in as many formats as you wish, but new rules issued by the ISBN AGENCY state that each version (i.e., format) of an e-book has to be allocated its own ISBN. The main e-book formats at the moment include PDF, AZW (the KINDLE uses this format), MOBIPOCKET and EPUB. Often, e-book readers will read more than one format, but some will read only one format.

In addition, you still need to market your e-book, and ensure that it can be distributed to the main e-book download sites via specialist firms who distribute e-books to the INTERNET

RETAILERS. You also need to check that your e-book is in a format that cannot be easily copied and printed. In the UK, GARDNERS have a 'digital warehouse' through which they supply many of the major retailers with e-books. They do not, at the time of writing, supply Waterstone's e-book store however.

The increasing interest in e-books has revived the discussion in publishing of DIGITAL RIGHTS MANAGEMENT (DRM). The publishing industry is also trying to price e-books correctly—making them appealing to consumers while taking into account the discounts that e-book retailers will receive (current thinking is that this has to be less than current TRADE DISCOUNTS for physical books). E-books are beginning to appear on the websites of the main retailers. Waterstone's now have a dedicated e-book store, with many other retailers soon intending to launch online stores. Waterstone's have linked up with Sony and have made the SONY READER their device of choice, with Borders choosing to sell the ILIAD. Other retailers like Blackwell and Foyles are following suit with e-books.

E-BOOK READER

A handheld device that will allow you to store and read e-books. The launch of Amazon's KINDLE (until recently limited to the USA), the SONY READER and the ILIAD—all of which retail for about £200.00 at the time of writing—offer the end user increased choice. E-book readers will allow you to store and download hundreds of new titles, they aim to replicate the 'look and feel' of a book, with backlit, 'paper effect' screens. A drawback to the e-book market at the moment is that the main e-book readers use different formats, so it is difficult for publishers to know which FORMAT to follow. Mobile phone manufacturers are also getting involved within the e-book market and starting to offer products that can be read on mobile phones. For example, there is now an application ('app') for Apple's iPhone that allows users to read e-books.

EPUB

ePub is a non-proprietary E-BOOK READER format, favoured by the big hitters like Sony, who use the format for their e-book reader (the SONY READER). To create ePub files, typesetting files or PDF files are converted into the non-proprietary XML format, and from there into the ePub format. Files created in ePub can then be easily converted into other formats suitable for different readers. Creating and converting files into formats suitable for e-books is a technical and complex process, and is best left to those with the programing skills required. See also E-BOOKS.

EAN 13

A unique product identifying number used in addition to the ISBN within the European supply chain.

EASONS

The leading books wholesaler in the Republic of Ireland, largely supplying bookshops in Ireland. .

EDI

EDI (Electronic Data Interchange) is a computer-to-computer

exchange of information designed to minimise human error and to speed up the SUPPLY CHAIN. Larger WHOLESALERS and stores use EDI to communicate ordering information to their trading partners. Most self-publishers will not be involved with EDI, as they will not have the necessary systems in place to handle EDI communications.

EDITOR

In a MAINSTREAM PUBLISHING house, the editor is central to the publishing process. Not only does the editor work closely with the author to shape the book, but they are often instrumental in acquiring a book initially. Self-publishing authors often act as their own 'editor', shaping the story as they wish; however, the closer you are to your work, the harder it can be to see the errors or flaws in the plot. Grammar and spelling errors can be rectified by recruiting friends, family members or professional copy editors at the proof checking stages, but problems with the flow of the narrative or story will be harder to spot—kindly and supportive family members may be unable or unwilling to tell you about them.

If you are using a SELF-PUBLISHING SERVICES PROVIDER you need to be aware that few will 'edit' a book in the same way as a mainstream publishing house (they may instead offer COPY EDIT and PROOF READING services). Grammar and spelling checks may or may not be carried out, but the bulk of the 'editing' will fall to you. Self-publishing companies or printers are highly unlikely to work with an author to improve the editorial content of a book. Experienced editors can be found to work with you before submitting for publication, but that will have an obvious cost implication. There are many companies that offer editorial services like this to authors, some more reputable than others. Shop around and get personal recommendations!

EMBARGO

In the books trade, some key titles have a sales embargo put on them. This means that retailers are not allowed to sell them before the date given, to avoid any one store having an unfair retail advantage. Embargoes can also be put on PRESS RELEASES—ensuring that news is not 'broken' before a given date and time (this can sometimes be, for example, because a deal has been done with serialisation in a major newspaper, and that newspaper insists on having an embargo so that no other paper can 'break' the story. It is not common for self-published books to work to an embargo—but it is worth noting that some WHOLESALERS and online sellers may not sell your book until the PUBLICATION DATE has been reached—even if they have stock or orders waiting.

EMBEDDING FONTS

If you are creating your own PRINT READY files, usually in Adobe's PDF format, you must embed any fonts into that PDF file when creating it from your typesetting software. Just because you have particular fonts present on your computer does not mean that the printer will have the same fonts—there are thousands and thousands of different fonts available, and even a straightforward font like Times will differ between font manufacturers. If you do not embed your fonts into your print files, you may find that the missing fonts are automatically substituted at the printers, either for a font that has the same name but which may be subtly different, or for something completely different (commonly Courier). This can lead to horrendous printing errors which will be your responsibility. Usually when creating a PDF file there is an option given in the print dialogue box to embed fonts, but different software works differently, so you may have to find out how to embed fonts from your software manual.

EMBOSSING

A way of raising an area—of text or an image—to add interest and texture to a book cover. Embossing is achieved by putting a book's cover or DUST JACKET through a press that has a raised area which pushes a part of the cover from the rear of the cover outwards, causing it to be raised on the front. Embossing cannot usually be done for books printed 'on demand' via DIGITAL PRINTING, though some digital printers can add embossing for longer digital print runs. If you want to have embossing on your book, it will have a cost implication for you, and you'll need to supply an extra file when you submit the book to the printers which shows exactly what should be embossed (if you want to emboss your book's title, for instance, then your embossing file will need to show only that area).

END MATTER

The items at the back of a book, such as an index,

bibliography, author biography, appendices, which do not form part of the book's main text. Not all books have end matter—novels often simply end with the last word of the story, or 'The end'.

END PAPERS

The end papers form part of the binding of a cased book. They are stuck onto the inside of the hard board covers, and carry through to form the first page of the book. End papers are often left blank, but you can have them printed to give extra decoration. For example, end papers may have a marbled effect, or can be used to carry a map or other relevant information. Printers will assume that end papers are to be left blank, so if you do want them printed on, ensure that this forms part of your quote.

ENDORSEMENTS

Quotes from well known people, or specialists within a field, used on a book cover and on a book's marketing materials to help drive book sales. Some people may ask for a fee for endorsing a book. To obtain an endorsement, you will need to approach the person (or persons) whom you wish to comment on your book, and you will need to send them a copy of your MANUSCRIPT if they agree to do so. This is best done after typesetting, so that the person in question can see the book in its final form. It is courteous to allow someone who has agreed to endorse your book at least four weeks to read and comment, so ensure that you have allowed for this additional time when drawing up your production schedule. See ADVANCE COPIES.

EPOS

Electronic Point of Sale, essentially the computer-based cash till of a bookstore, through which all sales are made and recorded. By scanning the BARCODES of all products sold, the store can keep tabs on prices, stock flow and takings. This is why it is essential to have a barcode on your book if you want retailers to sell it for you. See also NIELSEN BOOKSCAN.

EPS

Encapsulated PostScript, a file format often used to supply graphics files. EPS files are usually high resolution and thus large in size.

ESPRESSO

An in-store DIGITAL PRINTER that is being trialled in Blackwell. The Espresso stores thousands of books as digital files, and can then print a copy of a book while a purchaser waits. The machine is able to go from a customer order to a printed book in less than half an hour. The thinking behind Espresso is that a bookshop can only stock a finite amount of titles, and because retail space costs money, each book they stock has to 'earn' its shelf space. However, bookshops know customers want to purchase non-stock items, and the Espresso is designed to bridge this gap. The first machine was placed in the Charing Cross branch of Blackwell in 2009, with further machines due to be installed elsewhere if the trial is successful. The Espresso is run in conjunction with LIGHTNING SOURCE, who are making the PRINT READY files available.

ESTIMATE

A company's opinion of the projected costs of undertaking specific work on your behalf. SELF-PUBLISHING SERVICES PROVIDERS will estimate based on the criteria you have supplied. So this could be simply undertaking a CRITICAL ASSESSMENT of your manuscript or it may be a estimation of entire cost of getting your book produced, printed, marketed and distributed. Some self-publishing firms offer set price PACKAGES, others estimate each job on a bespoke basis. An estimate often forms part of the CONTRACT. Estimates are also called QUOTES.

EXTENT

The page extent is the number of pages in a book, including all of the PRELIMS and END MATTER. Due to the way in which LITHOGRAPHIC PRINTING works, you may find that you will have up to seven blank pages at the end of your book—most printers work in multiples of eight, printing in 8-, 16- or 32-page sections, and it is cheaper for them to simply leave any blanks that fall at the end of the book in the last printed section than to remove them.

The page extent of a book cannot be worked out until the book has actually been typeset, proofed and signed off as ready for printing. Only then can the extent be confirmed. Anything up to that point is either an ESTIMATE or an unconfirmed page extent. As the cost of most printing is based on the number of pages in the book to be printed, the final cost of printing cannot be confirmed until the final page extent is confirmed. In addition, the page extent (along with the weight and type of paper used) determines the width of the book (SPINE). For this reason, the book's cover or DUST JACKET artwork cannot be finalised until the page extent has been confirmed.

F

FINISHING

This is the term applied to the processes that happen at a printers once a book has been printed. It covers tasks such as folding, trimming, LAMINATING and BINDING. Once your book comes off the printing presses, it goes on to be 'finished'. DIGITALLY PRINTED books are 'finished' as part of the DIGITAL PRINTING process itself, but books printed with LITHOGRAPHIC PRINTING may be sub-contracted by the printers to a specialist company.

FIRM ORDER

A retail order made by a bookseller or WHOLESALER which is for a confirmed sale. This means that if the books are not sold, they cannot be returned to you for a refund. The other (more common) type of book order is SALE OR RETURN (SOR). With SOR orders, the wholesaler or bookseller can return the books to you for a full refund up to 9 months after they were ordered. It is all about RISK—and the booksellers usually don't want to take the risk of ordering books that they do not know they can sell. Sadly, sale or return is common in the book industry, and if you refuse to deal in SOR sales then you will find that your orders are severely curtailed.

FOIL

Foil is used to stamp the title and author (and imprint logo, etc.) onto hard cover case bound books, or it can be used on the covers of paperbacks to add a touch of luxury. You can select a variety of foils in different colours to enhance the look of a case bound book, though gold and silver foil are used most often.

FOLIO

A folio refers to a single page.

FONT

Fonts are divided into serif fonts (which have little tags on the ends of strokes—fonts like Times and Garamond), and sans-serif fonts (like Helvetica and Gill), which don't. Generally, serif fonts are easier to read if there's a lot of text; sans-serif fonts are usually used for titles and headings. However, there is no set rule. Fonts can be used to set the scene (in novels, letters and emails are often set in different fonts to the rest of the text, sometimes different character narratives are in different fonts, etc.). Some fonts are particularly good for covers (they are known as 'display fonts'), and others are highly unsuitable. Too many different fonts used in a project looks messy, and should be avoided. A common mistake in self-publishing is to make the font size (known as the 'point' size) too small, to try and make the book shorter (and therefore cheaper to print), or to use too large a font to make the text appear longer. Generally, 10 or 11 point size is about right for most projects. Your computer will come supplied with certain fonts, but there are many places where you can purchase other fonts online, with thousands available.

FORMAT

Format usually refers to the physical size of a book (the height and width). Books tend to be printed at one of a few standard sizes—publishers do not randomly pick dimensions and apply those to a book. Instead, they select a format that will suit the product, market and budget. For example, A-format books are usually 110mm x 178mm, B-format books usually measure 129mm x 198mm. Trade paperbacks are often similar sizes to their hardback equivalent, and priced more cheaply. B-format books are also sometimes called trade paperbacks, but B-format is traditionally used for more litcrary titles, which are often designed with wide margins, in contrast to the more cramped, mass market style of A-format.

A-format books are much cheaper to produce, printed in greater quantities and expected to sell well at a relatively low cover price in airport shops, supermarkets and bookshops. A-format books grew out of the 'pocket' book format established in the early days of mass market paperbacks, at a time when hardbacks were still the main event of the publishing world. The price of mass market fiction will be competitive, firstly because the publisher will print it in bulk, but also because the quality of the paper and binding are lower than that for other books.

In addition to these formats, there are other standard book sizes:

- Demy: 216mm x140mm, a larger sized format for novels
- Royal: 256mm x134mm, often used for non-fiction books
- Others formats include Crown, Octavo, Pinched Crown,

These all have different genres associated with them—Demy and Royal sizes are industry standard sizes that give the best size:cost ratio for printing, for example.

While market forces that make mainstream publishers select certain formats for certain titles are less likely to apply to self-publishers, it is worth considering that readers and retailers alike are consciously (or subconsciously) used to taking clues about a book's style and genre from the format. They would expect to see a literary fiction book in B- or demy-format, and a 'bodice-ripping' thriller as an A-format book. The type of book will usually dictate a format to you. A full colour coffee table book looks silly if novel-sized, and a novel looks very odd if it is A4 size, etc. Getting the format right is the first key decision when deciding how your book will look, and it is best to try to stick with formats that have been tried and tested over the years. When you are a bestselling author, then you can experiment and push the boundaries!

In the era of e-books, format now also refers to type of software or file used to create an E-BOOK.

FORMATTING

The format of a book refers to its size (height and width). If you are using a TYPESETTING service you will need to specify a size to them—a SELF-PUBLISHING SERVICES PROVIDER will have already quoted based on a certain format (size) of book, and if you are formatting the book yourself you will need to set your word processing (or typesetting software) template up at the right dimensions before you begin. When thinking about the size of your book, decide which size would be most appropriate for your work. Visit libraries and bookshops (or your own book shelves) and measure similarly themed books. The industry has standard sizes, which are standard because they are the most economical to print. See FORMAT for an overview of the standard sizes within the books trade.

FRONTLIST

The lead titles of a publishing company, and often the most heavily marketed and promoted. See also BACKLIST.

FRONT MATTER

See PRELIMS.

FSC

(Forest Stewardship Council)

A not-for-profit organisation that campaigns for the responsible use of the world's forests. You will often see books printed on paper that has been accredited by the FSC (and the book will usually display the FSC logo in the PRELIMS pages or on the back cover). Using this logo shows readers that the book has been printed on paper from accredited and well managed forestry sources. Using well managed sources may actually be more environmentally sound than using recycled paper in books. See BLEACH and PAPER.

FULFILMENT

The act of fulfiling a book order. See SUPPLY CHAIN and DISTRIBUTOR.

G

GALLEY PROOF

A galley proof is a proof of a book that has been typeset but not yet 'laid out' on the page. Nowadays it is unlikely that galley proofs will be produced by a typesetter, as it is common practice to typeset the text and handle the page layout as one overall process.

GARDNERS

One of the leading book WHOLESALERS in the UK. You are advised to make sure they have advanced information about your book—and to open an account with them, especially if you want to sell to Waterstone's stores. If you are not handling your own distribution, make sure your chosen distributor *does* have an account with Gardners. Gardners supply many independent and chain bookshops who use Gardlink to check stock and place orders. Gardners have launched a digital warehouse which retails E-BOOKS.

GHOST WRITER

A professional writer who will take your story idea and write it up, fleshing out the ideas to make a readable text. Celebrity autobiographies are often written with the help of a 'ghost'.

It is more unusual for ghost writers to be used by self-publishers, but if you do opt to use one there are contractual obligations that need to be discussed, not least the matter of whether or not they'll be entitled to any ROYALTIES, or if they will get a flat fee payment for the work instead.

GIF
A type of image format, see GRAPHIC FORMATS.

GOOGLE BOOK SEARCH
You can sign up to join the Google Book Search program which, like the AMAZON LOOK INSIDE scheme, allows potential browsers to search online a restricted number of pages within your book to help them decide if they want to buy it. There are restrictions upon what is made viewable, so the entire book is not readable or downloadable. Joining Google Book Search will give your book a higher ranking and visibility on Google itself, as Google will pick up hits from the entire text, rather than just from the title, author or ISBN. As of 2009, online bookseller The Book Depository use Google Book Search to allow potential customers to browse certain titles before buying.

Google cannot digitise books that are within COPYRIGHT without the copyright holder's permission. Many publishers send either electronic files or a copy to be scanned of each book they publish. However, the issue of digitisation is a controversial one, and at the time of writing, many authors and publishers are not happy with the Google system, preferring to opt out of the Book Search programme. With a big court case pending in the US over this, the ins and outs of this system are likely to change in the near future.

GRAPHIC FORMATS

Graphics files can be saved in several formats. The most common are .jpg (or .jpeg), .tiff and .gif, with .eps and .png also well known. For photographs or illustrations, the best formats to use are tiff and jpeg. The differences between the formats are as follows:

- Jpeg (.jpg)—a popular graphics storage method, used as the default image format by most digital cameras. It compresses the images, allowing larger images to be stored as smaller files. It is one of the standard formats for sending and storing images, but has a drawback; the quality of the saved image degrades each time it is resaved (making it a 'lossy' format). Jpegs are good for photos and greyscale images, but are not recommended for archiving due to their 'lossy' nature.
- Tiff—unlike jpeg, tiff is a non-lossy format, meaning that no degradation of an image occurs when it is saved and resaved, therefore making it ideal for archiving images.
- Gif is good for web-based graphics, but it has limitations in colour work, so it is not recommended for use with print-based applications.

When supplying a printer with graphics, make sure that you ask what format they prefer, and what RESOLUTION (usually 300dpi).

GSM

Grams per Square Metre, refers to the 'weight' of the PAPER and board that your book will be printed on. Typical weights are 80gsm for novels, 130gsm for glossy photograph pages, and 230gsm for paperback book covers. Printers usually stock some standard weights of paper, but will have to order in anything that they do not normally hold in stock from a paper merchant. When the paper weight reaches more than about 260gsm it is usually seen as 'card'.

GUTTER

The inside margin, situated on the bound edge of a book. The inside margin needs to have more space than the other margins to accommodate the BINDING, with between 2mm and 10mm required as extra space where the pages are glued into the SPINE. See also MARGINS.

H

HALFTONES

A halftone image is made up of a series of dots rather than as a continuously smooth image. Newspapers and magazines use halftone images (look at a photo in a newspaper closely and you will see that it is made up of small dots), and images within books are also usually halftones. They are used because printing produces minuscule dots of ink, using far less ink than if it printed using solids, and the eye is easily fooled by these tiny dots, interpreting them as a continuous image. Printers will usually check any images supplied by you and let you know whether your pictures are acceptable for good halftone reproduction.

HARDBACK

Hardback books come in two basic forms; either a hardback book with a wrap-around dust jacket (case bound), or a hardback with the cover stuck to the hard boards (printed paper case, PPC). In either case, the cover is made up of a thick card insert, the thickness of which is measured in microns, which is attached to the BOOK BLOCK with END PAPERS. A PPC cover will have a printed cover attached to the outside of the board. A case bound book will have

BLOCKING on the SPINE and possibly the front cover (usually in gold or silver FOIL), and a printed DUST JACKET wrapped around it. See FORMAT.

HARD COPY

A printed version of a MANUSCRIPT.

ILIAD

A portable E-BOOK READER that can read EPUB and PDF formats, among others. The Iliad was supported by Borders and retails for about £300.00 at the time of writing. See E-BOOK READERS.

ILLUSTRATION/ILLUSTRATOR

Some books benefit from having illustrations (and some books, like those for small children, will almost certainly require them). If you are not gifted artistically, then you will need to hire an illustrator. You and the illustrator will need to discuss terms and conditions, and agree prices. You need to be aware that you will need to pay for the work an illustrator has done for you even if you decide not to use their work. Also, you will need to think about who will own the COPYRIGHT to the illustrations, and how the illustrator is to be credited in the book—and paid—and whether they will receive ROYALTIES. Some illustrators will be happy to charge on a per job basis, and you as the artwork commissioner will then own the artwork. Others prefer to take a fee and a percentage of royalties from sales of your book. Be careful that you own the rights to the artwork produced, as some illustrators prefer to retain copyright to their work, which restricts you in future usage of that work.

When commissioning an illustrator, make sure you choose one that will be able to produce something in the style you want. Prepare a detailed brief of exactly what you want shown in each illustration, and ask to see roughs before the illustrator prepares final artwork. Roughs should be simple drawings that show you things like a picture's composition, how a character looks, and what they are doing. Changes should be made to the illustrations at this stage, not after the illustrator has prepared the final artwork.

IMPRINT

An imprint is the publishing name under which a book is published. If you are self-publishing and using an ISBN that you have acquired from the ISBN AGENCY, you will need to give a 'name' to your publishing imprint when you buy the ISBNs. If you are using a SELF-PUBLISHING SERVICES PROVIDER who is supplying you with an ISBN, you will find that your book is published under their imprint. Commercial publishers often have more than one imprint where, for instance, they publish fiction under one imprint, sport under another, books on dancing under a third, etc.

INSPECTION COPY

Bookshops or WHOLESALERS will sometimes ask you to provide an inspection or EVALUATION copy before they opt to stock a book. It is up to you if you wish to provide an inspection copy for a bookseller (they would not expect to pay for one). In academic/educational publishing, teachers and lecturers will often ask for an inspection copy (sometimes called an EVALUATION or desk copy). Giving such copies on request is common practice in MAINSTREAM PUBLISHING, but can be costly to a self-publishing author. Most lecturers will not expect to be invoiced for an inspection copy, though some publishers do apply terms and conditions to inspection copies, such as requesting that such copies are returned within 28 days in mint condition or an invoice will be sent. See also ADVANCE COPIES.

IN STOCK

Books that can be supplied immediately to a retailer or WHOLESALER from stock.

INTERNET RETAILER

Many people now choose to buy books from internet retailers. They do this for many reasons, convenience, choice and price being the main ones. In recent years, many high street booksellers have also developed an Internet bookselling presence, but dedicated online sellers such as AMAZON are the giants in this area. Internet stores can offer an almost unlimited selection of books—and a far wider range than could be stocked in a high street shop (where shelf space is an issue). It is worth noting that many online sellers will source books from WHOLESALERS, most do not actually have copies of your book in stock themselves. Therefore if you do not have accounts with wholesalers, it may be hard for internet retailers to get hold of your book to fulfil orders. The online booksellers, by making unlimited choice available, are actually helping self-publishers reach a wider audience and, potentially, assisting them to sell more copies. See the LONG TAIL.

ISBN

International Standard Book Number. An ISBN is a unique product identifier, that is specific to your book. From January 1st 2007, the ISBN became a 13 digit number (it was previously 10 digits long). All ISBNs now consist of the digits '978' preceding a unique publisher's identification prefix, plus a two-digit number to identify each title, then a check digit calculated from the previous digits. Every book published and sold through the books trade needs an ISBN, and these can be purchased from the ISBN AGENCY. It is not possible to buy just one ISBN, the minimum you can purchase is 10. If you are working with a SELF-PUBLISHING SERVICES PROVIDER, they can usually supply you with an ISBN as part of the package offered (and therefore they take over the duties associated with supplying BIBLIOGRAPHIC DATA). Remember that responsibilities come with ISBNs (see LEGAL DEPOSIT, NIELSEN BOOKDATA) and that you become the 'publisher' when you buy ISBNs in your own name or in the name of your own IMPRINT.

When you apply for your ISBNs from the ISBN Agency, you will have to fill in a form and send payment—10 numbers cost about £108 at the time of writing. Thereafter, on BIBLIOGRAPHIC DATABASES, those ISBNs will be associated with you. Orders will be directed to you through the prefix contained within the ISBN, unless you specify for orders to go to another DISTRIBUTOR when you apply for your ISBNs. There are very clear rules about what you can and can't do with an ISBN, which can be found on the agency's website *www.isbn.nielsenbook.co.uk*.

If you use an ISBN supplied by a self-publishing services provider, that ISBN, while assigned to your book, will (as far as the ISBN Agency is concerned) belong to the self-publishing company who paid for the ISBN prefixes. The self-publishing firm is likely to handle all the updating of bibliographic data as well. If so, you as the author will not be able to claim that ISBN for yourself, or directly make changes to the bibliographic record in the future, unless you are marked down as the distributor for the title and you deal with the orders that come in.

If you are acquiring your own ISBNs you will be issued with an ISBN log book. This lists all of the ISBNs you own. To register your titles with NIELSEN BOOKDATA—essential if you want anyone to be able to order the title—you will need to fill in one of the forms that was sent to you with your ISBNs (or you can submit information via email). Bibliographic data is important—getting it wrong can lead to missed sales and ordering confusion. The books trade will base their information about your book on the data you supply, and it can be hard to rectify errors later. It takes a couple of weeks, once you've submitted information to BookData for the information to filter through to the booksellers' websites and systems, so try to get your data sent in as soon as you can.

ISBN 13

In 2007, the ISBN became a 13 digit number. Until then it had been a 10 digit number. Since then, WHOLESALERS, bookshops and DATA AGGREGATORS have used the 13 digit number in their systems. You will often see ISBN 13 written on orders and forms, which indicates that the 13 digit number is the one now being used in the SUPPLY CHAIN. If you self-published your book before January 2007, you will probably have been using the 10 digit ISBN, which you will now need to convert to a 13 digit number. You can do this quite easily by using the free ISBN converter on the website *www.isbn.org/converter pub.asp.*

ISBN AGENCY

The ISBN agency is run by NIELSEN. It sells ISBNs and offers guidance on ISBN usage. Their website can be found at: *www.isbn.nielsenbook.co.uk.* See also ISBN.

ISSN

International Standard Serial Number is the equivalent of an ISBN, but for magazines and periodicals. All serialised publications should have an ISSN to allow easy identification and ordering. They work in much the same way as ISBNs.

J

JACKET

A jacket is either a book's card cover or a hardback's DUST COVER. Jackets usually carry the BLURB on the back or on the inside flap.

JPEG or JPG

See GRAPHICS FORMATS.

K

KINDLE

The E-BOOK READER designed and sold by AMAZON. It is now available in the United States and the UK. The Kindle is unique as an e-book reader (at the moment) in that you can download books wirelessly from Amazon. Most other e-book readers currently require a physical computer connection.

The Kindle can read several E-BOOK formats, including MOBIPOCKET and EPUB, but the main format (designed for it) is AWZ.

L

LAMINATION/LAMINATE
A thin plastic coating applied to the outside of book covers to increase durability. Matt and gloss laminate are the most popular finishes, with silk also being available. Unlaminated covers generally tend to mark easily, and often smudge.

You can combine laminates on a cover, by using spot lamination, which can be used as part of the overall design of a cover, rather than just as a protective coating. See SPOT LAMINATION.

LANDSCAPE
Landscape is a book format which is wider than it is deep (long top and bottom, shorter sides). Coffee table and art books—and some children's picture books—are often produced in landscape format. Landscape books are often costlier to print because the binding edge is the shorter edge, and thus if the book is heavy the bound edge will need to be stronger to take the weight. See also PORTRAIT.

LAUNCH DATE
See PUBLICATION DATE.

LAYOUT

The process of taking the various textual and graphical elements of a book and placing them onto the blank page to create the book, usually to a pre-agreed style. Layout designs can be very simple, such as the text in a novel, or very complicated, such as when using tables, pictures, graphs, captions, text and other design elements all on the same page. Page layout is a skilled design process that involves more than just slapping various things onto a page to fill it; if you are intending to prepare your own page layout, start by looking at lots of other books to see what others have done. Consistency is the key, and there are plenty of other rules involved in layout that are there because they work. If you have no experience of page design and layout and have a complicated book to prepare, seek assistance. See FORMATTING.

LEAD TIME

In book production terms, the lead time is the time lapse between a book being accepted for publication and it becoming available to sell. In trade buying terms the lead time is the time lapse between a publisher providing trade buyers with details of a new title and it becoming available to sell—trade BOOK BUYERS make buying decisions up to six months in advance, so publishers must provide information early to meet this (see BUYING CALENDERS). In publicity terms a lead time might be required by a newspaper or magazine prior to the PUBLICATION DATE being reached (i.e., some newspapers and magazines stipulate that REVIEW COPIES must be received by them up to three months ahead of their publication date—therefore the lead-in time would be three months).

LEGAL DEPOSIT

It is a legal requirement for UK publishers to deposit six copies of each title they publish that carries an ISBN (or ISSN) with the BRITISH LIBRARY NATIONAL BOOK COLLECTION (NBC). One copy is sent to the British Library Archives, now in Scotland (formerly in Wetherby, Yorkshire). The other five are sent to the Copyright Library Agent in London. These books are then distributed to Cambridge University Library, the Bodlean Library, Oxford, the National Library of Wales, the National Library of Scotland, and the National Library of of Ireland. Publishers can be prosecuted if they fail to deposit legal copies. If using a SELF-PUBLISHING SERVICE PROVIDER who has supplied you with an ISBN, check to see who is responsible for the legal deposit of your book. If you own your ISBNs you will need to deposit your own books.

LETTER OF AGREEMENT

Sometimes letters of agreement are used (in place of a CONTRACT) if you are contracting the services of another party to undertake publishing work for you. A supplier may ask you to sign a letter of agreement (or sometimes, a letter of intent) instead of a contract, which will state the key factors of the agreement between you and that company. It should include reference to the price, the services you are using and possibly a publication date and royalty agreement. Again, check this carefully before signing and if the QUOTE forms part of the letter of agreement, check that as well.

LIBEL

Libel refers to the writing or publishing of something that sets out to discredit another person without justification. (Slander is the equivalent in the spoken word.) Self-publishers need to be careful—especially if writing factual accounts of events in the recent past, or writing fiction that is really thinly veiled fact. It is often not enough to just change the name of someone that you are writing about—if a person feels that they can still be identified in a 'fiction' and that discredits them publicly, they may still have a solid case in law. People who feel they have been libelled have recourse to the law, and may seek substantial damages. If you are in doubt about whether something that you may have included in your book could be libellous, seek legal advice.

LIBRARIES

Libraries usually buy books either through LIBRARY SUPPLIERS or through buying consortia. Rarely will a library have a budget of its own with which it can buy books direct from a publisher or author. Often, a library will buy several copies of a book so that branches within the same local district can have a copy in each, and this is particularly the case for books with a local interest. You can find out from your local library where to send information on your book so that it can be considered for purchase.

LIBRARY SUPPLIERS

Library suppliers are companies who source and sell books to libraries, both general and academic. Certain titles (crime fiction, for example) will sell better through a library supplier because that genre is popular in public lending. University libraries (i.e., academic libraries which supply the research publications that their students/staff need), tend to get their books from specialist academic library suppliers. Many of the library suppliers are now part of the main book WHOLESALERS, and are therefore able ask for the same TRADE DISCOUNTS off the cover price as the wholesalers themselves receive. See also BRITISH LIBRARY and PUBLIC LENDING RIGHT.

LIGHTNING SOURCE

The UK's largest print on demand DIGITAL PRINTER. They now print over 2 million books per year, but they do not offer any self-publishing services (such as design or TYPESETTING). If you are a publisher you can apply to be a customer and, if successful, you can then upload and print books from PDF files via their online system. Lightning Source can also distribute books that they print, create E-BOOK files and are also the key partner in the ESPRESSO book machine.

LIMP BINDING

See BINDING.

LITERARY AGENT

An agent acts for the author when negotiating with publishers over selling a MANUSCRIPT for publication. Getting an agent is extremely difficult, and would-be authors can often find that MAINSTREAM PUBLISHING houses will only consider submissions that come from authors with agents. Agents are looking out for titles that have a ready market, and above all that they can sell to a publisher. Yet even having an agent is no guarantee that your book will find a commercial publisher.

Self-published authors need to be aware of non-reputable 'agents' who ask for payments in advance so that they can to represent them, or who ask for payment to have manuscripts critically assessed before signing up a book. Reputable agents do not ask for payments from authors, they make their money by selling books to publishers and taking a percentage of any sales fee and ROYALTIES. Good agents can be found in the *Writers' & Artists' Yearbook* and on the website of *The Association of Authors' Agents—www.agentsassoc.co.uk*.

LITERARY SCOUT
Literary scouts seek out new writing talent, and new writers within popular (i.e., good selling) genres. They also look out for books that fit into recent publishing trends and books published in other languages that will do well in a different market (eg. European books that would have a market in the USA). Scouts differ from agents in that they do not manage authors and their RIGHTS; they seek out the books that publishers would want to publish and authors that agents will wish to represent.

LITHOGRAPHIC PRINTING (LITHO)
Books requiring a larger number of copies (+500) to be printed are usually printed using traditional ink and presses with rollers (much as you see newspapers being printed). Paper

is fed through the presses either from a roll (roll-fed) or in sheets (sheet-fed) over the printing plates and through rollers. Litho presses usually print either 8-, 16- or 32-up, which means that they print 8-, 16- or 32-page sections of a book on each pass through a press. Each section is then folded and trimmed to make an 8-, 16- or 32-page section, with several sections gathered together to form the entire BOOK BLOCK.

The set up costs for litho printing are higher than those for DIGITAL PRINTING because litho presses need printing plates, onto which each page is transferred in reverse. Once the plates are on the presses, the cost to the printer is the time it takes to print the requisite number of copies and the paper required. The UNIT COSTS for longer PRINT RUNS are therefore lower the more copies of a book you print in one go. Litho printing becomes more cost effective than DIGITAL PRINTING for print runs of around 500 and over, although this figure is changing all the time with developments within digital printing.

LONG RUN

A long run refers to a PRINT RUN of anything over 500 copies. Due to efficiencies of scale, long run books are mostly printed using LITHOGRAPHIC PRINTING methods.

LONG TAIL

The long tail theory was put forward by Chris Anderson in his seminal book *The Long Tail*, which examines how the internet has led to 'unlimited choice'. His theory touches upon book sales (and self-publishing), and considers how the internet should make it simpler for self-publishers to sell (and produce) books—and how it has made it easier to reach niche markets. Anderson takes as a starting point the concept of a bricks and mortar bookstore which can stock, say, a maximum of 20,000 titles due to shelf space limitations. Taking into account that each title with shelf space has to help pay the store overheads (rent, wages, equipment), the store owner can't afford to stock anything that will be more 'niche' and not sell regularly (i.e., books by lesser known authors, books about minority topics). Anderson then compares this setup to an online store which has far fewer overheads and can still offer the big titles (the 'hits' guaranteed to make money), but can also, because of the low overheads and the necessity of not having to hold stock, sell the 'long tail' niche titles. Interestingly, Anderson estimates that about a third of Amazon's sales are 'long tail sales'—i.e., sales that would not have happened in a conventional bookstore, but which when added together make up a large amount of revenue. You will find references to the long tail creeping into many articles and 'thinking' about publishing at the moment, and so you may find it useful to have an overview of this theory. Anderson's latest theory touches up the concept of 'free'—and how giving content away can lead to sales. See INTERNET RETAILERS.

M

M/S, m/s, MS or ms
Common abbreviations for the term manuscript. See MANUSCRIPT.

MAILING LIST
A list of people potentially interested in your product that you send MARKETING information to via post or email. You can buy mailing lists in almost every subject area, or you can collate your own. Before you start mailing anyone (via email or post) you need to make sure you are not breaking any data protection rules. If you purchase a list, you need to ensure the list has been collected with the recipients' permission. If you are putting together your own marketing lists, then you need to follow some rules—such as only using contact details for people who have agreed to let you contact them. There are some exceptions to this (for example, if they are being contacted as they have expressed interest in similar products or if they are being contacted but have a simple way to opt out of future communication). For more specific information about this issue, see the useful pages on data protection here: *www.ico.gov.uk/Home/for_organisations/ topic_specific_guides/marketing.aspx*

MAINSTREAM PUBLISHING

Under a mainstream publishing arrangement, the publisher will own the RIGHTS to an author's work and will have control over the entire publishing process. In return, they take the financial RISK on publishing the book, and pay the author a fixed ROYALTY and ADVANCE on those royalties. This is also referred to as traditional publishing.

MANUSCRIPT

A manuscript is the raw text of a book prior to its publication in book form. 'Typescript' and 'manuscript' are now often used interchangeably. Historically, a 'manuscript' referred to anything written by hand, whereas typescripts were typed.

MARGINS

When positioned on a book's page, the text should not run too close to the edge of that page. The white space between the edge of the text and the edge of the book's page is called the margin. It is tempting for self-publishers to make the margins in their book as small as possible, thereby getting more text on each page, and thus fewer pages overall—which is cheaper to print. Yet by doing this, you can make a book look really cramped and unattractive. Packing text onto a page will make the margins look mean and the book hard to read.

Also, bear in mind that the book is going to be bound—do not make your inner margins too small, otherwise the text can be too tight at the bound edge, making reading it impossible. Margins should ideally look the same all the way around once bound, but there will, by necessity, be a larger margin on the bound edge (usually called the GUTTER) to allow for the BINDING process.

MARKETING

Marketing is the process of informing potential buyers about a product, in the hope that they will decide to buy it. In the books trade, marketing is directed towards WHOLESALERS and retailers, as well as to the the target readership.

Self-publishers can also market to the books trade as well as straight at their potential readership. For example, marketing a book on cine film can be done relatively easily to a local cinema club. Marketing a novel is, paradoxically, harder as the potential readership is far wider in both geographical and interest terms.

Marketing is a generic term which encompasses all sorts of activities, from putting up a simple poster or handing out a flyer, to sending out ADVANCE INFORMATION sheets and PRESS RELEASES, REVIEW COPIES and BLADS. Very often it is impossible to quantify the effect that any one marketing activity may have on the sales of a book. However, if no marketing is carried out then a book is unlikely to sell well at all.

For self-publishers, marketing is often the hardest part of the publishing process. All publishers have to work hard to make their products stand out in a very crowded market, and self-publishers have to work twice as hard. Some SELF-PUBLISHING

SERVICES PROVIDERS will offer advice on marketing, others offer tangible help in the form of producing posters and leaflets, and a few will actually market books in the same way as any commercial publisher. Ensure that you are aware of exactly what will be carried out by way of marketing if you are considering using a services supplier in this way.

Publishing a book can be done quite simply nowadays, but actually getting it into the hands of those in the retail trade who make the decisions on whether or not to stock a book is far harder. For example, the retailer WH Smith is notoriously reluctant to take any book that is not backed by a substantial marketing campaign or some form of marketing 'assistance' to the retailer. Most retailers are just as interested in what marketing activities will be undertaken as in the book itself, particularly if it is by an unknown author. Set your marketing goals realistically and don't imagine that it will be easy.

MASS MARKET PAPERBACK
See FORMAT.

MEDIA PACK
Magazines and newspapers—which take advertising—will usually have a media pack. This pack gives an overview of the publication, its circulation figures and RATE CARD (which lists the cost of ADVERTISING in that publication).

METALLIC INK
Metallic ink gives a metal-effect by increasing the reflectivity

of ink through the addition of small particles of metal. Metallic ink is not the same as FOIL. Take advice from your printer if you want to use metallic ink, as there are some factors which impact on how it will look in a final project (such as what LAMINATE you use, the paper or board used in the project, and its impact on other inks). Metallic inks can only be used when printing on LITHOGRAPHIC PRINTING presses; DIGITAL PRINTING cannot print with metallic finishes yet.

MID-LIST

A term for authors whose sales are respectable rather than bestselling. Mid-list authors can be vulnerable when a mainstream publisher decides to reduce its lists.

MOBIPOCKET

An e-book format. See E-BOOKS.

N

NET BOOK AGREEMENT (NBA)

Established on 1st January 1900, the Net Book Agreement (NBA) was a voluntary publishers' agreement which allowed them to set a minimum price for a book. Discounting was only allowed under certain schemes (eg. book clubs, library and school supply). The NBA has now been abolished and no longer applies to the UK, therefore whatever cover price you set is only a suggestion, a RECOMMENDED RETAIL PRICE. Bookshops can sell your book for whatever price they wish, neither the publisher nor author have any say over the matter. Thus, you may find that your book is being sold at a heavily discounted price by some retailers, and for less than you may be selling it yourself. This is because retailers receive a TRADE DISCOUNT on the cover price from the publisher, which can sometimes as high as 60%. From within this discount, the retailer can decide to pass some or all of it on to their customer.

NIELSEN

A UK company providing essential services to the books trade, which includes the ISBN AGENCY (which allocates ISBNs), NIELSEN BOOKDATA (which keeps BIBLIOGRAPHIC DATA records), NIELSEN BOOKNET (which sends book orders to publishers via TELEORDERING) and NIELSEN BOOKSCAN (which provides sales and analysis information).

NIELSEN BOOKDATA (NBD)

The main BIBLIOGRAPHIC DATABASE supplying information to the books trade. You can simply send them a form with your book's BIBLIOGRAPHIC DATA on it, or if you wish, you can subscribe to PubWeb, Nielsen's online title management system that enables you to input data online. All shops, whether physical or online, take their data from Nielsen BookData, so any book on their database with them will find its way onto all bibliographic databases, including Amazon.co.uk.

If you are using an ISBN supplied by a SELF-PUBLISHING SERVICES PROVIDER then they will deal with bibliographic data on your behalf. If you have purchased your own ISBNs, you will need to tell Nielsen Bookdata about your books yourself.

Making your bibliographic data available via BookData technically means that your book will be available to buy through many thousands of retailers. In practice, however, merely being present on a bibliographic database and on retailers' bibliographic lists does not necessarily mean that a single copy will be sold, not without some form of MARKETING to draw the retailers' or readers' attention to the book.

NIELSEN BOOKNET

A service run by NIELSEN that routes orders electronically from retailer to supplier via TELEORDERING. If you are handling your own distribution, you may receive teleorders from shops and WHOLESALERS. They are usually sent via email.

NIELSEN BOOKSCAN

By tracking sales from over 8000 UK book retailers, BookScan is the most accurate record of book sales in the UK. Nielsen BookScan sales information is used to compile bestseller charts, and can also be accessed by companies who subscribe to the service (such a publishing houses who use it to track their book sales via bookshops, and can use that information to make decisions about their publishing strategy). Not all publishers subscribe to the service. As the data is collected for sales that go though a cash till (see EPOS) of a participating store, self-publishers may find that the service is not much use to them, partly because many self-publishers' sales are direct to readers so do not register on the retailers' figures, and partly because , in reality, the levels of sales are unlikely to register in Nielsen's figures.

NOTCH BINDING

See BINDING

NOT YET PUBLISHED (NYP)

A book that is in production but that has not yet been printed. See also AVAILABILITY STATUS CODE. Retailers will still place orders for books that have not yet been printed, and these are held on DUES until the books are ready.

0

OFFSET PRINTING

A printing technique whereby ink is spread onto a metal or paper plate with etched images, and then transferred to a rubber blanket, and finally to the paper. Offset printing (also known as LITHOGRAPHIC PRINTING) is used to produce large PRINT RUNS. The set-up costs are relatively high for offset printing, but once set-up, the more copies you print, the lower the UNIT COST will become.

ONIX

The data exchange standard used within the books trade for sending computer-to-computer information about books, thereby increasing the accuracy and timeliness of the data transmitted. Data sent using Onix covers a wide spectrum of book information—from BIBLIOGRAPHIC DATA to RIGHTS and licensing information, thereby allowing publishers to deliver information rich data to WHOLESALERS, BIBLIOGRAPHIC DATABASES and other suppliers

At the moment very few SELF-PUBLISHING SERVICES PROVIDERS supply bibliographic data in ONIX format, though the larger publishers do.

ONLINE BOOKSHOPS
See INTERNET RETAILERS.

OPTIONS
You may hear of some books having had a film 'option' taken out on them—this does not guarantee that a film will be made, just that someone has 'reserved' the RIGHTS (for a set time) to make it into a film if they can. Mainstream publishers sometimes take the 'option' on an author's next book—giving them the first option on publishing the new book. In both cases, the authors would receive some financial recompense for the options taken on their work, even if the final project does not come to fruition.

OUT OF PRINT (OOP or OP)
An abbreviation meaning that a book is no longer available to buy and there are currently no plans to reprint it. You (or whoever deals with your BIBLIOGRAPHIC DATA) must notify the DATA AGGREGATORS when a book falls out of print so that the books trade can be informed and cease ordering it.

OUT OF REGISTER
This is a printing error sometimes found in colour LITHOGRAPHIC PRINTING work. It occurs when OVERPRINTING. If the presses get 'out of register' it means that on each pass through the press the printing plates did not print in the exact same place, thus the colours are slightly offset from one another, giving the printed pages a fuzzy or blurred effect. If you think your book has been poorly printed in this way, you

need to take it up with the printing firm. This is an error at the printing press, not a fault in the files that were supplied to the printer. If some of your books are affected, it does not mean that all of your books are—the press could have become out of register at any point during the run.

OVERPRINTING

Colour printing carried out by LITHOGRAPHIC printers uses a four-colour printing process. Four colours (Cyan, Magenta, Yellow and Black—known as CMYK) are printed one on top of the other to make up all the other colours. The pages of a colour book printed in this way effectively pass through the printing press four times, one for each colour. The marks that are found on colour proofs are CROP MARKS which guide the printers in ensuring that the four different colours match up exactly.

OVERS

Copies of a book printed by the printer over and above those ordered by the publisher/author. LITHOGRAPHIC printers will usually print up to 5% extra so that if there are any copies damaged on the BINDING line, or by ink smudges on the presses, or if copies are damaged in transit, then they have already printed copies to replace these. This is cheaper for the printing firm than having to reprint a very small number of replacement copies. Any copies that are printed over and above those ordered may be charged for by the printers, but if there are more than 5% overs you can ask for them to be pulped so that you do not have to pay for them.

P

PAGE

This may seem an obvious one, but what exactly is a page? A page is a single side of a sheet of PAPER, it is not a single sheet of paper (with two sides). If a book is estimated to have 100 pages in it, that is pages numbered from 1 through to 100, that would mean 50 sheets of paper printed on both sides. Printers will charge for printing partly on the number of pages in a book, so make sure you realise that they are talking about both sides of a sheet of paper as an individual page, rather than each sheet of paper itself. Pages can also be called FOLIOS.

PANTONE COLOURS

A colour matching system which allows you to specify exact colours to printers. It gives the reassurance of having a colour reproduced as you would expect to see it, but it also means that, in addition to using the CMYK colours, you will have to pay more to also print using a specified Pantone colour (as this will be another pass through the press for the paper).

PAPER

Papers are classified by weights and types. Standard papers

for printing are usually between 80gsm and 130gsm in weight; what you will most commonly see in a novel is 80gsm paper. GSM stands for 'grams per square metre'. The weight of the paper can affect the project in a number of ways. For example, the paper weight can have an impact on the SPINE width of a book (printers have scales and charts which show them the page EXTENT and paper weight, which will allow them to calculate spine width). Choosing the right paper is important. For example, novels are often printed on BOOKWOVE—a cream or white textured paper that is cost effective and flexible. Photographic books and art books are often printed on COATED PAPER that works better with graphics. The thicker the paper, the more ungainly the BINDING can be. Ask to see a sample of the paper your printer is proposing to print on. If you have been quoted for printing on a certain type of paper, ensure you are happy with it before approving the job, as selecting a different paper may alter the print costs. Papers that are acid free will last longer and do not discolour as much.

Paperback book covers are printed on card, which is thicker than paper (typically, covers are on board between 230gsm and 300gsm). Again, check what you have been quoted for— really stiff cover board can make a book hard to open and read, yet board that is too thin can make the book floppy and the cover arc open when the book is lying flat.

Papers can also have colours, the most common being the cream bookwove papers and white art papers, but there are many others available (including textured boards for covers).

If you are using DIGITAL PRINTING, you will often be limited to a smaller choice of papers. In LITHOGRAPHIC PRINTING, you should be able to choose from a wide range of paper options.

The publishing and printing industry has—in recent years—been conscious of the environmental impact of paper use, and often now offers FSC papers or recycled papers (that need bleaching). See FSC and BLEACH. Both may well add to the cost of your print bill.

PAPERBACK
See FORMAT.

PAPER STOCK
If you see 'paper stock' written on a quote, this indicates the type of paper that the printer is proposing to print the book on. See PAPER.

PARTNERSHIP PUBLISHING
Some SELF-PUBLISHING SERVICES PROVIDERS offer a 'partnership publishing' programme. All schemes vary, but often it means the self-publishing firm and the author 'split' the investment, and therefore the RISK, involved in publishing. It is hard to generalise about the different packages available, so look into this carefully if you are interested, and check exactly what is on offer. Don't get over-excited by an offer of partnership publishing deal until you are sure that there is a fair split of risk and ROYALTIES—and that you are willing to share any success with your partner firm!

PASS FOR PRESS

You will often be asked to sign your proofs off before the printers (or SELF-PUBLISHING SERVICES PROVIDER) will start printing your book. This generally means that you have checked your typeset proofs and are accepting responsibility for any remaining errors in the text or on the cover. If uploading files to an online printing firm, accepting the TERMS AND CONDITIONS on upload usually amounts to the same thing. Don't approve something as ready for printing and then start to make changes! You should only sign something as ready for print when you are absolutely sure it is ready for print. Making changes after you have signed a Pass for Press form is likely to lead to additional charges from either the printer or your self-publishing provider.

PDF

Portable Document Format (PDF) is a file format created by Adobe Systems for document exchange. PDF is used for representing printed documents in a way that is independent of the software, hardware or computer operating system used to prepare the original files. Each PDF file includes a complete description of a fixed-layout document, including text, FONTS and images. As it is platform- and machine-independent, PDF has become the *de facto* standard for print, in both DIGITAL PRINTING and LITHOGRAPHIC PRINTING. Virtually all printers accept PDF files as print-ready files as they are fixed format.

PDF files can be created in many common applications, like Microsoft Word. However there are limitations, and to ensure correct print output the PDF files themselves must have the fonts used to create them embedded within them. If you are arranging printing yourself, ask your printer to perform a 'pre-flight check' on your PDF files. This will throw up any problems or potentially poor images that are used in your file before the book is printed.

If you supply faulty PDF files to a printer it is your responsibility, not theirs, if the resulting book is incorrect. Printers do not alter PDF files, they are fixed, so any errors contained within them will remain in the printed book.

PER COPY PRICE

The price that each copy of a book has cost you to produce. This is not the same as the price you sell the book for. Working out the per copy price will help you to work out a selling price (RECOMMENDED RETAIL PRICE, RRP), and a break even point, taking book TRADE DISCOUNTS into consideration. See UNIT COST.

PERFECT BINDING

See BINDING.

PERMISSIONS

The granting of permission (in writing) to reproduce an article, poem, song, etc. from the original COPYRIGHT holder.

PICA

A unit of measurement in the printing/typesetting industries that is equal to 1/6th of an inch.

PICTURE LIBRARIES

These are image banks, usually viewable online, where images are available to buy for use in your projects. There are two types of image library: managed rights and royalty free:

- Managed rights are images where the fee you pay is based upon the individual project. There are restrictions on the number of times you can use the image, and in what context. Essentially, you are granted license to use the image for a specific project.
- Royalty free images are images you pay a one-off fee to use in your project. There are still restrictions on the image's use, however, and you are not buying the image outright, you are buying a licence to use it in a project.

Picture libraries allow you to download low RESOLUTION 'comp' (i.e., trial) images to try out in your designs. If you are happy with the image, you can then go and buy it to get a high print resolution version. You cannot simply download an image and use it without paying, as this is a breach of COPYRIGHT. Most picture libraries use their company logo as a watermark in a 'comp' image, and only when you buy an image will this watermark be removed. They do this to prevent people from using images without permission, while still allowing you to try out images in design projects.

PIXELS

See RESOLUTION.

PLATES

Used in LITHOGRAPHIC PRINTING and made from either metal or paper sheets, imprinted with the negative of a book. The paper runs over the plates on the printing press and prints a positive image of the book onto the paper. See also OFFSET PRINTING.

POINT

The FONT size. Most books are set in 11pt or 12pt type, with chapter openings and cross-headers being in a larger font, and RUNNING HEADS in a smaller size. The point sizes of different fonts will not always look the same, with some being much bigger than others, so do not assume that because you specify a certain point size that it will be the size you want it to be.

PORTRAIT

Portrait is a book FORMAT that it is deeper than it is wide (like a novel, or a painted portrait). See also LANDSCAPE.

POSTSCRIPT

Postscript is a page description language created by Adobe Systems that describes a page's text and graphical content, and which was a precursor to the more commonly used PDF format. PDF files are in fact often created by printing a document to Postscript format, and then running the resulting Postscript file through Acrobat Distiller. This then gives a high quality PDF file ready for printing. If you do not have Acrobat Distiller (which is a paid for software program), then you may be able to print your files to Postscript format and send these to the printers for conversion into PDF files.

PRELIMS

Prelims refers to the opening pages of a book, before the main text itself starts. Prelims are sometimes referred to as front matter. The *prelim*inary pages of a book generally have their own convention standards:

- First right-hand page – the Half Title page (contains the title only; or sometimes an author biography on its own).
- First left-hand page – usually left blank.
- Second right-hand page – the Full Title page (to include subtitle, author name and IMPRINT).
- Second left-hand page – here you often find publishing details, including publisher information, PUBLICATION DATE, COPYRIGHT information and printer's details.
- Third right-hand page – contents, acknowledgments or dedication.
- There will follow a blank left hand page, then items such as a foreword, preface, introduction and contents list usually form part of the prelim pages as well, rather than the main body of the work itself.

The prelim pages should be numbered using roman numerals (a publishing convention) not arabic ('normal') numbers. Blank pages, are counted as part of the pagination, but it looks better if there is no physical page number on the page itself (try to avoid any RUNNING HEADS on blank pages too). As a guide, pick up any mainstream published book and look at the prelims to give yourself an idea of what they should look like and how the pagination has been handled. Self-published books often have insufficient or incorrect prelim pages, with information packed in too tightly.

Remember that the prelims are the reader's first experience of your text, so don't cram everything in—books always look better with some space left in the typographical design.

PRE-PRESS WORK

Pre-press effectively refers to all of the work that needs to be done to a MANUSCRIPT to get it ready for printing. This can include the obvious things like COPY EDITING, TYPESETTING and cover design, but may also involve things like commissioning an illustrator, arranging for advance endorsements and assigning an ISBN.

PRESS RELEASE

Written specifically for the media, a Press Release (PR) contains important book and author information, and is an essential tool for MARKETING your book. Good PRs should not just give a synopsis of the book, but find a 'news' angle that the press can connect with. Sometimes PRs are sent out at the same time as REVIEW COPIES. You need to target your PRs carefully, don't go for a scatter-gun effect, it doesn't work. One sheet of A4 paper with crucial information about your book and how the press can contact you should be sufficient. You may also find it beneficial to have different versions of your PR, depending on whom you are targeting and the news angle—for example, a local PR will have a different emphasis than one for the national press.

PRINTED PAPER CASE (PPC)

See BINDING.

PRINT ON DEMAND (PoD)

See DIGITAL PRINTING for an expanded overview. Digital technology that allows for the economical printing of very small numbers of books. Print on Demand can even be used to print a single copy of a book when the demand arises, removing the need for holding stock. See DIGITAL PRINTING for an expanded overview. PoD is a good way to get a book into print in very small numbers at a relatively small cost, but it is limited when it comes to being suitable for selling books into mainstream retail. Because the printer is printing a single copy of the book, the UNIT COST is far higher than if you printed, say, 100 copies in one go. Some PoD companies will assign a very high cover price to a book that is far outside what a customer would expect to pay simply because the sale of the book would otherwise bring in less than it cost to print. Self-published books in particular often suffer from having an unrealistically high cover price—a standard paperback novel priced at £13.95 will simply not sell well, because people expect novels be priced at around £8.

PoD is used by major publishers when the book in question has a high cover price, for example an academic textbook or a non-fiction book with a specialist audience. In such a situation PoD can work extremely well. But as a self-publisher, be sure that your book is not being priced out of the market before it is even published.

PRINT READY FILES

These are files that are ready to send to the printers. Usually PDF files, but (depending on the printer) you can also send files as Word, XPress or InDesign. The printer will then make them into PDFs for you. See PDF and CAMERA READY COPY.

PRINT RUN

The number of copies of a book that are printed in any one go (a print run of 500 copies should give you approximately 500 books—if you don't ask for a run on with your print order you may end up with slightly fewer (see OVERS); if you do ask for a run on then you will probably end up with more copies, but you may be charged for them. Printers will often print more copies than you order so that any problems that occur while BINDING or finishing don't leave them short on your order.

PRINTER'S PROOFS

These are proofs of your book sent out by the printer before a book is bound. Printer's proofs are not sent so that the text can be read and checked, that should have been done already, either by you or by a proof reader. Printer's proofs are sent so that you can check that the printer is outputting what was expected, in the correct order, and that pictures are clear and colours (if used) are correct.

If using DIGITAL PRINTING, it is possible to order just one proof copy of the complete book to check before placing a larger order. If there is an error in the proof copy then you can upload new files (usually for a fee) and order another copy. If you change things after your printer has generated proofs then they may well make an additional charge, because they are likely to have incurred additional cost through no fault of theirs.

PRINTER'S SCALES

Printers often have a scale of charges to print a book based around common FORMATS and finishes. The scales may also indicate things such as likely SPINE widths based on paper volume and page extents.

PROCESS COLOURS

These are the four colours used in printing full colour, CMYK (Cyan, Magenta, Yellow and Black) from which you can make up about 90% of all other colours. When working in colour and printing within LITHOGRAPHIC PRINTING, you will need to convert images from RGB (Red, Green, Blue) to CMYK, otherwise, when the printers output proofs, the colours may be different, as litho printing is done in CMYK not RGB. Most home PCs/Macs are set up to use RGB as a default because that is how monitors and TV sets display colour, whereas printers want colour files (including covers) as CMYK. See also SPOT COLOUR. DIGITAL PRINTING can use either RGB or CMYK COLOUR SEPARATIONS as they do not print using the four process colours.

PROOFS

There are different kinds of proofs—from the proofs you read through yourself (author proofs) to check for errors in the TYPESETTING and design process and the marked up proofs that you may receive back from a proof reader, to the different types of PRINTER'S PROOFS (such as GALLEY PROOFS, output proofs and the BOOK BLOCK). If you are using a DIGITAL PRINTING firm you may find you do not get printer's proofs, instead you can order one copy of the finished book to check that it has printed as expected. If it has not, you will need to upload revised files (usually for an extra charge).

Author or galley proofs are part of the process of putting a book together. They are not set in stone, so if there is something that needs changing, don't panic! Just ask your typesetter to amend the proofs. Output proofs and book blocks are, however, a different matter as these are proofs of the actual printed books and changing them means submitting and printing new files.

PROOF READING

The act of checking a book for errors once it has been typeset. Before everything was done on a computer, typeset proofs were checked against the original MANUSCRIPT, but nowadays it is likely that the original manuscript is already in a format like Word, and that it has been used as the basis of the TYPESETTING. There are thus likely to be fewer typesetting errors. Proofs are generally checked after typesetting as a last chance to spot errors in the text or problems in layout that the typesetting process has caused.

PRO-FORMA INVOICE

An invoice that must be paid in advance of goods being

dispatched—sometimes issued by printers. You can also issue pro-forma invoices if you want payment upfront for book orders (which is advisable if supplying abroad), or to customers unknown to you, who order small numbers of books.

PSD

A .psd file is a file generated by the graphics software Adobe Photoshop. If you have used a designer to work on a project for you, you may encounter .psd files. In these files, all of the images and text are embedded in an editable file in different layers. Psd files are not flattened (i.e., all the picture and text 'layers' have not been compressed into one). If, for example, you are using a cover designer to prepare a cover design, but a SELF-PUBLISHING SERVICES PROVIDER to put your book together, you may be asked to supply the cover .psd file to the self-publishing services firm for finalising before print. Therefore, it is worth making sure that your designer keeps a copy of the .psd file, rather than just sending a final, flattened, cover image to which no changes can easily be made.

PUBLICATION ABANDONED (AB)

You will need to notify NIELSEN BOOKDATA if you have decided not to go ahead with the publication of a book after you have notified them of the BIBLIOGRAPHIC DATA. Nielsen will then update their records to show that the publication never happened, so the books trade will know not to place orders and the BRITISH LIBRARY will not chase you for LEGAL DEPOSIT copies.

PUBLICATION DATE

This is the date that the book is ready to be released for sale. It is not necessarily the date that you can expect to have your book back from the printers. In MAINSTREAM PUBLISHING, the publication date may be some time after the books have been printed. This allows the publicity departments to get the ball rolling with press and media interest. It also allow for the SUPPLY CHAIN to creak into action, getting books shipped out to where they need to be.

It is generally understood that books will not be sold by retailers until the publication date has been reached—thus allowing you to get copies out to shops for launch dates. For self-publishers, it is good to set a publication date that is some time after the actual books have arrived, because this gives you valuable extra time. If the book encounters problems at the printers, for example, having extra time before the official publication date can help to minimise stress. It gives you time to get the MARKETING of your book underway, and it allows time for the books trade to feed updated information about your book through the system so that a book is shown as available, as opposed to forthcoming, on the BIBLIOGRAPHIC DATABASES, shop websites, etc.

It causes less stress to wait until you have your books before organising any book launch events. It sounds counter-intuitive, but once the books arrive you can go ahead and make what plans you want, secure in the knowledge that you won't be standing at the front of a crowded room with no book to show.

PUBLICATION DELAY

This occurs when a book is published after the advertised PUBLICATION DATE. You'll need to tell anyone who has ordered the book, and inform services such a NIELSEN BOOKDATA if you have a publication delay. This is sometimes also known as a slipped publication date.

PUBLIC LENDING RIGHT (PLR)

Authors registered for the PLR scheme receive payment for the borrowing of their books through UK public libraries. Payment is made based on the number of times your book is borrowed from a sample of libraries (not from every library). To learn more and to register, go to *www.plr.uk.com*. If you are not registered you will not receive payment, and as the author the onus is on you to register, a publisher cannot do it for you.

PUBLISHING AGREEMENTS

These are CONTRACTS between MAINSTREAM PUBLISHING houses and authors. Most self-publishing firms and services providers offer simpler CONTRACT or TERMS AND CONDITIONS than one might find in a 'publishing agreement'. This is because when you sign up with a self-publishing company, you are buying their expertise to get the book produced, and perhaps, marketed. The 'rights' of the work and the license to use them should remain with you as the author. In mainstream publishing, the author is selling the publisher the use of the RIGHTS of the work for a period of time, and the author will get an ADVANCE payment and a ROYALTY paid in a different way as a result. A publishing agreement looks in detail at this rather than the actual task of producing a book.

PUBLISHING PACKAGES

Many people who self-publish enlist the help of a SELF-PUBLISHING SERVICES PROVIDER. Some choose to use 'PACKAGES' which a lot of companies offer. These are usually called things like gold, platinum and bronze packages, and they can be an effective way for people to self-publish. However, make sure that you compare the many different publishers' packages, and look carefully at all the small print. Sometimes things that are included in packages (such as listing your book on Amazon.co.uk and online bookshops) are actually things that happen automatically for any book with an ISBN, so you should not be paying more for them.

Some self-publishing firms offer a bespoke service, rather than packages. This allows for a more flexible approach to your project. It simply comes down to what will best suit you and your book. It can take time to compare service providers as each company will offer something a little different, but it will be time well spent if you research them carefully.

PUBLISH ON DEMAND

See PRINT ON DEMAND AND DIGITAL PRINTING.

PULPING

This is the process of 'destroying' a book and removing it from sale. If it becomes necessary to pulp any of your books, look into ways of doing this through firms that specialise in bulk paper recycling, as you really want to remove the books from the SUPPLY CHAIN.

$\mathcal{Q}$

QUOTE

A quote is usually an ESTIMATE (based on the criteria you supply) of the projected costs of getting your book produced and/or printed. It may be that you are just seeking a print quote, or perhaps you are seeking a quotation for a company to take your MANUSCRIPT and turn it into a book and market it. To fully understand a quote, you may need to look up individual terms in this book to ensure that the quote you have received matches your requirements.

Typically, printing quotes will be based on the dimensions of a book (FORMAT) the number of pages (page EXTENT), BINDING, colour printing (if applicable), the type of PAPER used within the book and the paper or board for the cover. It is important to note that printing books is VAT exempt, but PRE-PRESS work (design, typesetting etc.) will be VAT chargeable, and you will need to budget for it if you are using a company to do your pre-press work for you.

At the quote stage you need to decide what you want and to specify exactly that when requesting a quote... printers especially will base their quote or estimate on the book specifications you supply them with. If you specify the wrong materials or finish, then it is your problem if the book does not turn out how you expect.

Here is a list of the items a printer or SELF-PUBLISHING SERVICES PROVIDER will need to quote for your book:

Printing specification checklist
* the number of copies you want,
* the binding type,
* the paper type,
* the number of pages your book will make when typeset (the page extent),
* the type of LAMINATION (matt, gloss, etc.) you require,
* if you are printing in colour.

A quote for the pre-press work (i.e. the work that includes everything prior to going to print) will usually be for items such as TYPESETTING, the cover design, cover image research and purchase, PROOF READING, COPY EDITING etc. A firm that specialises solely in printing is unlikely to offer many of these services, so you will need to look elsewhere to have them done if you do not feel able to do them yourself. Self-publishing service providers generally do offer all of these services.

Pre-Press checklist
* do you require your book to be typeset?
* do you want an external proof read and/or copy edit?
* do you need a cover design (including or excluding image

acquisition)?

- do you need images scanning, the book typing up etc?

Some self-publishing services firms also offer MARKETING services. A quote for marketing can include items such as mailing ADVANCE INFORMATION (AI) sheets, PRESS RELEASES and REVIEW COPIES, the printing and design of marketing materials, or web pages. Again, you can opt to take a marketing package or you can do it all yourself. It is best to find out what the marketing entails if you use a marketing service as packages will vary.

The quote will often form the basis of a CONTRACT or agreement with a company, so if you change your mind later, your costs may increase. For printers and some self-publishing service providers, a quote is based on an estimate of how many pages a book will make when typeset, so if it makes substantially more or less pages once ready for print, the quote is likely to go up or down accordingly. Some self-publishing companies include items such as ISBN and cover design, some don't, so it is worth getting quotes from a variety of places.

Ideally, we recommend that you check back with the company if you are at all unsure about any particular item mentioned. Remember that every self-publishing service provider offers a slightly different service, so it is worth shopping around to see what best suits you. If you are technologically savvy, there is no reason why you cannot undertake a lot of the PRE-PRESS WORK and then send files to a printer, or upload them to a DIGITAL

PRINTING provider. Quite a few self-publishing service providers specialise only in PRINT ON DEMAND and DIGITAL PRINTING, so if you want a top quality book printed using LITHOGRAPHIC PRINTING, you need to check that this is what you are going to get. Also many self-publishing services providers offer PACKAGES or PARTNERSHIP style agreements, and again, it's worth having a look at what is on offer with more than one firm before signing up to a service.

The golden rule is never assume anything when getting a quote! Just because you 'thought' your book would be printed on a certain type of paper, doesn't mean it will be *unless* you specify exactly what you want. If you don't know what to specify, ask to see samples.

R

RATE CARD

The rate card lists the price of taking an advertisement in a specific publication or on a website. You can usually negotiate discounts off the advertised rates... regular advertisers rarely pay the ADVERTISING rates specified on the rate card. See MEDIA PACK.

REGISTRATION MARKS

See CROP MARKS.

RESOLUTION

A digital image is made up of pixels (small squares). Understanding image resolution (and therefore pixels) is important to ensure you get the best possible quality graphics. If you need images for a project that will be viewed online—then images need to be 96 DPI (dots per inch), or they will be too large to load quickly. If you are printing images in your book they must be at least 300 dpi.

Remember that the image must be 300 dpi at the size you need it, you cannot scale the size of a picture up because the resolution will degrade, making it poor quality when reproduced. For example, if you have a 300 dpi image but it is only one inch wide and you need to reproduce it at 8 inches wide, you cannot simply make the figure bigger as it will seriously compromise the quality. If you are uncertain how wide and high the image will need to be in your project, ensure it is scanned in (or made available to you) at 600 dpi to give you some leeway. The higher the resolution, the larger the file will be, but that is a small price to pay for having a usable image! It is important to ensure you have scanned in the images correctly at the start of the process. This is also why you cannot simply copy graphics off websites for use in your project (COPYRIGHT issues aside)—the image will be 96 dpi and much too small to be used for printing.

RETURNS

Books supplied on SALE OR RETURN (SOR) can be returned for full credit if unsold. The bookshop/WHOLESALER that wishes to return books may send a returns authorisation, which you may have to sign to agree to the returns. Most book trade sales are made on a SOR basis—although some PRINT ON DEMAND books are FIRM sale only.

REVIEW

Many self-publishers are eager for a review—but do not always appreciate that a review can be negative as well as positive! Reviews are very subjective, they are one person's view of a book. Some people tend to think of reviews only in the context of national magazines and newspapers, but influential reviews also appear on websites such as AMAZON, where people who have read/purchased a book can offer their feedback. Sometimes this feedback can be negative and, unless is it offensive of inaccurate, Amazon will not remove it... so you have to develop a thick skin.

It is now an offence to post a favourable review of your own book under a real or false name, so don't be tempted.

Rarely are self-published books reviewed in the national media, and when they are, it is usually because the book is about a 'hot' topic. It is difficult enough to get a review in a local or specialist publication, let alone a national daily. Be realistic about what to expect.

REVIEW COPIES

Free copies of your book will need to be sent out to the media and those who may be able to REVIEW or champion it. A review copy is a loss leader, you cannot send the review copy out and ask for it back if the title is not reviewed (you would be amazed how many people do!). Reviewers are usually unpaid, their only reward being the copy of the book they have reviewed. Be prepared to send out free review copies and build in the cost of doing so into your publishing budget.

RGB

See PROCESS COLOURS.

RIGHTS

An author initially owns all the rights to their MANUSCRIPT. If a mainstream publisher wishes to take a manuscript on, they must acquire some or all of the rights before it is possible for them to produce and sell a version of the work. The publisher who acquires the rights then has a license to use that work, or sell it, thus generating further income. In self-publishing, the author should retain all of the rights to the work themselves—even if they are using a SELF-PUBLISHING SERVICES PROVIDER to assist them to publish. A CONTRACT must be specific about the rights that an author is licensing to a publisher or publishing company. In self-publishing, for example, you should retain ALL of the rights, so make sure that any contract or letter of intent makes this very clear.

The main types of rights include:

- North American Rights – the rights to publish the work in the US and Canada.
- Translation rights – the right to translate the work into a different language.
- Electronic rights – the rights to the electronic format of books and their content. (Of course with the rise of the E-BOOK, things such as Electronic rights are becoming more important. Usually rights are are sold for specific platforms and for short periods.)

There are other rights like audio book, film and TV rights, and the rights to publish extracts from a work, all of which are negotiated in contracts. If you are self-publishing it is important to maintain your rights as it means that no one else can produce a legal version of your book. Also, should your work be picked up by a LITERARY AGENT or mainstream publisher, you are in a stronger negotiating position if you still own the rights.

Be aware that rights 'expire'. For example, if you sell the foreign language rights to your work, but the expected edition does not appear within the timeframe specified in your agreement, then the license is considered void and those rights will return to you (and no refunds for sold rights are given).

Other types of rights you might encounter are TERRITORIAL RIGHTS (the geographical 'areas' of the work for which you hold the publishing rights).

RISK

This refers to the financial risk present in publishing a book. If self-publishing, this is at the author's risk—i.e. there is no guarantee that you will make a profit from your book, or even get your investment back. Risk may be shared in PARTNERSHIP PUBLISHING schemes, but you need to understand how that risk is being shared in such arrangements. In MAINSTREAM PUBLISHING, the risk lies entirely with the publisher, and this is why publishers tend to play it safe and publish established genres/authors that they know they can sell. In bookselling, booksellers minimise their risk by taking books as SALE OR RETURN.

If you are self-publishing and thus funding publication of your book, never borrow money to pay for publication assuming that you will be able to repay that loan from sales receipts. Never invest more than you can afford to lose!

ROYALTIES

The percentage of the net or gross book cover price the author can expect to receive from sales once TRADE DISCOUNTS and other fees have been deducted. In self-publishing, you will have to allow for books trade discounts of between 35% and 60%, and if you are using a SELF-PUBLISHING SERVICES PROVIDER or DISTRIBUTOR to sell your books, you will have to deduct a further percentage fee—plus if your book is DIGITALLY PRINTED you will also need to deduct per copy print cost— before you can calculate royalties. The key to working out royalties is careful accounting. You need to know what each copy of the book has sold for before you can calculate the royalty you receive. If you are selling the book yourself—and you have all the copies—you will not receive royalties, but all receipts from your sales. If you are using a self-publishing services provider to distribute your book on your behalf, you'll need to know what percentage of each sale will be received by you—and when/how payments of royalties are due. (See UNIT COST.)

RRP

Recommended Retail Price, the suggested selling price of a book. Since the abolition of the NET BOOK AGREEMENT (NBA), this is a suggestion rather than an enforceable price, and you will see that shops often choose to discount the RRP to their customers.

RUNNING HEADS

Used at the top of a book's text. The recto (right-hand page) could be the section title, or author name, and possibly the page number. The verso (left-hand page) may be the book title (and possibly also page number); though there are no set standards really. Non-fiction usually has running heads, fiction may not have them, but there is no hard and fast rule. Over-large running heads can look cumbersome and, in some books—children's picture books, for instance—running heads are often omitted anyway. In some design-led books, running heads are used at the bottom of the page, not the top—it's all a matter of choice.

RUNNING SHEET

A running sheet is a printer's printed but unbound copy of a book's text. Lithographic printers often send a copy of the running sheets to the publisher as a final check before BINDING takes place. Digital printers don't supply running sheets.

S

SADDLE-STITCHED

See BINDING

SALE OR RETURN (SOR)

This is used to describe the terms on which a bookseller or WHOLESALER may order a title. Books sold on SOR can be returned to the publisher (or DISTRIBUTOR) by the bookseller for a full refund if they have not sold them within a given time frame (usually 6-9 months after ordering and paying for them or taking them on CONSIGNMENT), providing that the books are returned in a resaleable condition. Sometimes a returns authorisation must be signed by the publisher/distributor before the books can be returned, but if you agreed to supply on sale or return you cannot change your mind when the shop asks to return books.

SOR is not popular within the publishing industry in general, and there is talk of it being abolished in the future. This would possibly do a disservice to many small publishers, as bookshops who can't return stock for a refund are less likely to take a RISK on unknown/untried authors or publishers. A different (preferable for self-publishers, but less common) type of order is FIRM SALE. With firm sales, books cannot be returned if unsold, but you often have to give the bookseller a larger discount as a result. You will find that some shops will refuse to take copies, or take a smaller number of copies, if you refuse SOR terms. DIGITALLY PRINTED books are often supplied on firm sale only—and this can mean that fewer copies are likely to be sold through the books trade as a result; certainly far fewer copies will be bought by bookshops 'on spec' to sell on to customers.

SALES REPRESENTATION ('REPPING')

Mainstream publishers usually have a force of sales reps who cover distinct geographical areas, showing booksellers and WHOLESALERS new titles and seeking orders from them. Repping has declined somewhat in recent years, but many still see it as the only way to get books in front of the key decision makers. Self-publishers will often need to be their own sales rep—going to bookshops and showing their book.

There are companies who will take titles to rep into bookshops, chains and wholesalers, but this will be expensive (they may well take a percentage of the cover price or a flat fee), and there is no hard and fast guarantee of success. For DIGITALLY PRINTED self-published books it is likely that the profit margin would make repping impossible anyway.

Most SELF-PUBLISHING SERVICE PROVIDERS do not offer any form of sales representation to their authors. There are currently only two UK-based self-publishing companies that do; the Book Guild and Matador.

SANS-SERIF FONTS
See FONTS.

SELF-PUBLISHING
An author pays for the production of their own book and retains the RIGHTS and control over the process. Nowadays there are many SELF-PUBLISHING SERVICES PROVIDERS that can help you to self-publish your book for an agreed price, but of course it's also possible to become your own publisher and do the whole thing alone. For purists, self-publishing means that you do everything yourself, but as with any complex industry, it is near impossible to get to grips with the organisational, technical and complicated vagaries of how a book is produced, distributed and sold. For that reason, most 'self-published' books are published on behalf of the author by a self-publishing services provider, which carries out some or all of the work involved for a fee. The key issue here is that the author should have the last say on all aspects of their book's publication, and should retain all rights. See also VANITY PUBLISHING.

SELF-PUBLISHING SERVICES PROVIDER
A company that an author can contract to undertake some, or all, of the production, printing, MARKETING and distribution when self-publishing. Many firms offer full service self-publishing (they provide ISBNs, marketing and organise printing); others specialise in services such as PRE-PRESS WORK. Picking a reputable firm can take a little bit of research, but a good place to start is the annual *Writers' and Artists' Yearbook*.

See also VANITY PUBLISHING, PARTNERSHIP PUBLISHING and PACKAGES.

SERIAL RIGHTS

The sale of extracts from a book to a newspaper or magazine. Serial rights are negotiated between the publisher and the publication. Newspapers and magazines want original material to fill their pages, usually on an exclusive basis to protect their investment; this means that other publications cannot publish extracts until later on, as the work may be EMBARGOED. See RIGHTS.

SERIF FONTS

See FONTS.

SEWN BINDING

See BINDING.

SIGNED COPY

A copy of a book that the author has signed or annotated in some way. Sometimes signed books are worth more in a collectors' market. Signed books generally will be taken on FIRM SALE, not SALE OR RETURN by bookshops, so it's worth checking this before you sign all your copies!

SHORT RUN

A short run in printing is anything up to 500 copies printed in one go. It is usually more cost effective to print fewer than 500 copies using DIGITAL PRINTING—though this does depend on the book size and specifics. (Full colour work may still work out to be cheaper with LITHOGRAPHIC PRINTING.)

SHOW THROUGH

The amount of the preceding page that can be seen through the reverse of printed pages. This depends not only on the PAPER type but also on its density. Thinner papers will have more show through and do not stand up well to having heavy black graphics printed onto them as a result.

SLUSH PILE

Unsolicited MANUSCRIPTS sent to publishers and agents often find themselves on the slush pile. Sometimes readers do trawl though some of these manuscripts in the hope of finding something good, but generally publishers and LITERARY AGENTS prefer solicited manuscripts and urge prospective authors to follow their submission procedures. This usually means that you need an agent to represent you and your work when approaching publishers.

SOCIAL NETWORKING

Social networking is about community building and interacting online. Social networking websites include FaceBook, MySpace, and Twitter and social networking tools include Tweets (small text updates about what you are doing sent to anyone signed up to receive them) and Blogs. Social networking is, by and large, free and can, if used correctly, be a useful way for self-publishers to market their books to a potentially large audience. You will need to set up profiles on the main social networking websites and then then invite 'friends' to join your network. As with all such things, rules apply to stop the system being abused. There are social networking sites dedicated to most topics (Goodreads and Shelfari are ones dedicated to books and readers, for example), and LinkedIn is an important corporate and business networking scheme. Social networking sites are now a growing and large area—and many publishers are experimenting with using them for MARKETING books (though no one has yet reached any definitive conclusions about how effective this really is). See TWITTER.

SOFTBACK
See FORMAT.

SOFT COPY
An electronic copy of a MANUSCRIPT, held on a computer hard drive, disc, CD or on a memory stick.

SONY READER
A portable E-BOOK READER made by Sony. See E-BOOKS.

SPECIAL ORDER
Most books will not be held in stock by bookshops or WHOLESALERS, but instead will be ordered as required. These are known as special order items, and customers will need to request the book, rather than find it upon a bookshop bookshelf.

SPECIFICATION (OR SPEC)
The specifications for the book that form part of the QUOTE.

Printers use 'specs' to generate estimates or quotes for print jobs. Specifications include things like a book's physical size, paper type, cover finish, etc.

SPINE

The spine of a book is the part of the cover between the front and back covers! You usually have to have a minimum spine width (4mm) to be able to physically put text on the spine. It is best to print on the spine if possible as bookshops can't display every title with the front cover facing outwards; if the spine is left unprinted the book will be easily missed if displayed spine out.

During PRE-PRESS WORK, the spine width is calculated from the number of pages the book makes, the EXTENT x the PAPER weight. It is important to know the spine width of the book when working on the cover design, so the full COVER SPREAD can allow for the correct spine width. lithographic printers will usually be able to tell you a spine width, but if you are using a DIGITAL PRINTING service, you may need to calculate it yourself using their spine width calculators or by requesting a template.

SPOT COLOUR

Lithographic printers can print very specific colours using the PANTONE colour guide and specific inks. If your book absolutely must contain a specific colour, then you can specify that Pantone colour to the printers. If printing in full colour and with a spot colour, the print costs will be greater as it involves an additional run through the presses. Spot colour is often used inside a book to add interest to the text, especially in textbooks and similar publications. The text would then be printed in black and one spot colour.

SPOT LAMINATION

Also called spot UV. A shiny laminate added to a specified area on a book cover rather than the entire cover. This adds texture to a cover—offering you the chance to have a matt background with a selected gloss area (or vice versa). If you are having spot lamination done, you will need to provide a separate file showing the exact area that you wish to have spot varnished. DIGITAL PRINTERS can usually only offer gloss lamination on covers.

STITCHED BINDING

See BINDING.

STYLE SHEET

If you are using a company that offers TYPESETTING you may need to supply them with an idea of the FORMAT of the book and any specific typographical ideas that you have (i.e.,. 'I want all the figure captions to be in bold font', or 'I want every chapter to start on a right-hand page'). The company can then mock up a style for your approval.

This is important because typesetting a whole MANUSCRIPT to one style, and then being told that, actually, you'd rather use different FONTS or have line breaks not indents between paragraphs, means the entire book has to be retypeset (and usually at your cost). A style sheet (style proof or style guide) will apply a certain style to the first few chapters for your approval and then, once approved, it is this that can be tweaked and checked before the rest of the manuscript is worked on.

SUBMISSION

If you are submitting your MANUSCRIPT to a printing or SELF-PUBLISHING SERVICES PROVIDER for a QUOTE or for their consideration, *never* send the original and only version of your book! Find out if the company you are submitting to prefers to receive typescripts as soft or hard copy and submit appropriately. Put your contact details on the first page of the manuscript in case the covering letter or email goes astray. Make sure that you send the right file, and don't keep sending updated or different versions. It is always worth phoning to check the submission policy for self-publishing service providers before sending in your work. Specify in your covering letter what you want from the company you are sending your manuscript to—remember, they get lots of enquiries every day and, unless you specify what you require, they are not going to know what you are looking for.

SUBMISSION LETTER

The covering letter (or email if submitting electronically) that accompanies your submission to a publishing house or LITERARY AGENT. If you are sending your book through to a company that offers self-publishing services, it should state exactly why you are writing and which services you are interested in. If you want a QUOTE, ask for one. Make sure you put your contact details on the letter and state if you want the manuscript returning to you or not. Always check websites or phone and ask before submitting a manuscript to make sure that what you have submitted matches what they require.

SUBSCRIPTION SALES

These are pre-publication, advance trade sales for a book. Mainstream publishers use these to gauge the potential popularity of a book. As a self-publisher, you are more likely to get advance direct sales (from friends and family) than from the retail trade.

SUPPLY CHAIN

The supply chain encompasses all the stages from book orders to book delivery. There are are usually many different ways for a customer to get hold of a book: direct from the publisher via their website, via the Internet bookshops, buying the book in a bookshop off the shelves, ordering the book from a bookshop and having it delivered to that shop, plus now, in some shops the opportunity to order the book and have it printed for you on the ESPRESSO machine there and then. The supply chain can be complex—relationships go from publisher, to WHOLESALER to supplier and back. There are moves afoot to try to make as much of the supply chain electronic, and thus avoid waste (so orders will be sent via the internet) rather than posted or faxed. See EDI.

SWATCHBOOK

A book or strip of samples produced by product manufacturers that can show PAPER types and weights, METALLIC INKS, cloth and coloured papers for END PAPERS. PANTONE produce sample swatch books for colour-matching. etc. Your printer should be able to let you look at relevant swatchbooks if required—unless you are using a DIGITAL PRINTING service, where choice of paper, board, inks and bindings, etc. will be much reduced.

SYNOPSIS

A concise overview of a book's contents. A good synopsis can form the basis for MARKETING the book later. A synopsis should not be a blow by blow account of the book, but highlight the key points.

T

TELEORDERS

Orders taken by NIELSEN BOOKNET on a publisher's behalf and emailed/faxed over to publishers (or their DISTRIBUTOR) for fulfilment each day. If you go into a bookshop and make a SPECIAL ORDER (i.e., for a book they don't stock), they will usually look it up on their system and then place a teleorder direct to the publisher (or their distributor) for that title.

TEMPORARILY OUT OF STOCK (TOS)

Books that cannot immediately be supplied because they are temporarily unavailable (e.g., the book is being reprinted, etc). See AVAILABILITY STATUS CODES.

TERMS AND CONDITIONS

For printing firms, including many DIGITAL PRINTING companies where you upload your own content, your CONTRACT with them may be a set of terms and conditions which you will need to approve before the job will be undertaken. If uploading files to a digital service, check these terms—don't just click the 'I have read and understood the terms and conditions' check box until you actually have. For example, if you are using a service such as Lulu or LIGHTNING

SOURCE, the responsibility to upload correct files lies with you and extra charges will be made if your files are not formatted correctly. It is no good complaining if you uploaded incorrectly formatted files before reading the terms and conditions! See also CONTRACT and LETTER OF AGREEMENT.

TERRITORIAL RIGHTS

When you submit your BIBLIOGRAPHIC DATA, you will need to indicate what market you have the RIGHTS to sell your work within. Unless you have sold any rights to the book in question, you should indicate worldwide rights.

THIRD PARTY REPRESENTATION

There are third party companies that represent a publisher in selling that publisher's titles to the retail trade. So neither the author nor publisher is selling their own books, they employ someone else to do the active selling. SALES REPRESENTATION is usually carried out on a commission or fee basis, but companies are generally only interested if you have a list of books to sell, and more in the pipeline. Taking on a single book to sell is not cost-effective for such companies.

TIFF

See GRAPHIC FORMATS.

TRADE BUYERS

Buyers in the retailers and WHOLESALERS who make key book buying and stocking decisions. See BOOK BUYERS

TRADE DISCOUNT

See also TRADE TERMS and TRADE ORDERS. Trade discount refers to the amount given off the cover price to trade customers. Discounts range from 35%-60%, with AMAZON taking up to 60% (in some cases) and WHOLESALERS and large chains up to 45-55%.

TRADE ORDERS

Trade orders are orders made by a company whose main business is to sell/supply books (therefore all sales in the books trade are subject to a TRADE DISCOUNT). Trade orders are usually made by a retailer through a WHOLESALER or DISTRIBUTOR, but they may also be made direct to a publisher.

TRADE PAPERBACK

See FORMAT.

TRADE TERMS

The terms on which you do business with booksellers (i.e. trade customers). If you are asked to supply your trade terms the bookseller will expect to see the TRADE DISCOUNT you will give off the cover price, and whether you will charge postage or if you'll cover the delivery costs. Most will want to see that you offer SALE OR RETURN, and what your payment terms are (payment 30-60 days in arrears is common in the books trade).

TRADITIONAL PUBLISHING

The publisher owns the RIGHTS and has control of the entire

publishing process, making their money by selling a book, paying the author a fixed ROYALTY and an ADVANCE on those royalties. This is also referred to as MAINSTREAM PUBLISHING.

TRANSLATION RIGHTS
See RIGHTS.

TRIMMING
Once the pages are printed, they are trimmed to the required size before BINDING. Trimming can sometimes go awry and you may occasionally see books that have been trimmed incorrectly—on an angle, too close to the edge etc.

TWITTER
A SOCIAL NETWORKING tool that has seen a sudden growth in popularity in the last year. It's a free to use service that encourages frequent, short (no longer than 250 words) messages that are then sent to all your 'followers'. Many well known authors (Stephen Fry, for example) have huge Twitter followings, and publishers are using Twitter to market books. A message sent on Twitter is called a 'tweet'.

TYPEFACE
The FONT used in the typographical design of a book. See also POINT.

TYPESETTING
The process of putting a book into the correct layout ready

for proofing and printing. Also called 'setting'. Mainstream publishers use typesetting software (such as QuarkXpress or Adobe InDesign) for this. It's not common in the publishing world for books to be typeset in desktop publishing programmes such as Microsoft Word because they were not designed for typesetting. Although self-publishers, with a lack of industry software, usually use desktop packages like Word, it is true that the industry software offers much better and more accurate layout results. Remember that poorly designed and printed books will detract from good content, so if your book is being typeset, make sure that the standard of what is on offer is high enough. It is not always enough for a self-publisher or self-publishing company to simply format a Word document and expect it to compare well to a properly typeset book.

TYPING SERVICES
These services are undertaken by typists who can type a MANUSCRIPT up from a handwritten document, audio tapes or from a hard copy where the soft copy is corrupted or unavailable. Typists set their own rates, but usually the charge will be per page or per 1000 words typed up.

TYPO
A typographical error in the text.

U

UNIT COST/UNIT PRICE

When dealing with WHOLESALERS and bookshops, the unit cost refers to the price for *one copy of a book*. So if your book is priced at £6.99, its unit cost, before any discount, is £6.99. If you are asked (by a bookseller) for the unit price *after* discount, simply deduct the agreed discount percentage from the book's RECOMMENDED RETAIL PRICE (RRP), and quote that as the price per unit copy with discount.

However, unit cost has another meaning because the unit cost is also what YOU pay per book when you print/publish it. You will need to work out what the cost per unit (for each book) is. It's best to work this out at the start of the self-publishing process, because you need to know what the PRE-PRESS WORK + printing + extras equals so you can work out a RRP for your book. You don't want to set a RRP which means that, after production, printing and TRADE DISCOUNTS have been taken into account, you lose money on each book sale. On the other hand, you also need to realise that pricing a paperback novel at £13.00 is not going to result in many sales.

If you are having 100 books printed, and the production costs are £400.00, then you can work out that your unit cost (at cost price) for ONE book is £4.00. But with book trade discounts you will, as a worst case scenario, sell each book at a discount of 60%, so you will have to price your book at £10.00 just to break even.

Generally, the fewer books you print in one go, the higher the unit cost. So where a PRINT ON DEMAND book may cost £4 a copy to print, the same book may cost only £2.00 if you print 1000 copies in one go.

V

VANITY PUBLISHING

Vanity publishing is exactly what the name implies. An author publishes a book for reasons of pure vanity, to get their book into print. Up until about 2000, vanity publishing was also a term synonymous with 'rip-off' publishers charging a considerable amount of money to 'publish' a book but to make no attempt to actually sell it.

Following a high-profile campaign by the anti-vanity publishing campaigner Johnathon Clifford and the *Mirror* newspaper, many vanity publishers were exposed and put out of business. However, there are still a few companies around that will charge far more than is reasonable for a sub-standard service, so do your homework and obtain comparative QUOTES from different companies if you are thinking of using a SELF-PUBLISHING SERVICES PROVIDER. Make sure you know what you are getting for your money!

More information on Johnathon Clifford's continuing anti-vanity publishing campaign can be found online at *www.vanitypublishing.info*

VAT (VALUE ADDED TAX)

Book sales are exempt from VAT—as is the printing of books —*unless* the book has a CD, DVD or online content sold as part of the product, in which case VAT is applicable to that part of the product and must be paid. VAT is applicable to all the PRE-PRESS WORK done on a book as undertaken for you by a SELF-PUBLISHING SERVICES PROVIDER.

VIRAL MARKETING

A MARKETING tool that gains its own momentum and starts spreading your message to as wide an audience as possible. Often these are campaigns that are started via email or through SOCIAL NETWORKING sites, and they can lead to increased awareness of your book (and hopefully sales). The best viral campaigns are those that contain video or audio and appeal to people sufficiently for them to pass them along to their social network contacts (who in turn, you hope, will pass the message along to their contacts, etc).

W

WATERSTONE'S HUB

A new, centralized distribution depot for Waterstone's which opened fully in 2009 and that, in theory, allows them to supply all their shops and move stock around between stores (helping to reduce RETURNS). The hub initially experienced teething problems but at the time of writing these were being ironed out.

WEB 2.0

A word that describes how the 'second generation' of web design and development has changed how we use and perceive the internet. The web, as technology has increased and download speeds have improved, is now a place where we interact. As well as searching and researching we also upload, download, blog, tweet, post reviews, comment on reviews, upload and download images, music and video and network with other people. All of these facilities have changed how the web looks and feels, and how we think about the web—and this is what Web 2.0 is all about. Knowing that web users now like to participate in the sites they visit, think about what you can put onto your web site to enhance the user experience.

WHOLESALERS

Wholesalers supply books to the books trade (i.e. bookshops, gift shops, book clubs, internet bookshops, etc.). They buy from publishers at a TRADE DISCOUNT, and supply to the books trade on more competitive terms than an individual bookshop can usually get direct from a publisher. The two largest wholesalers in the UK are GARDNERS and BERTRAM BOOKS (who between them have over 80% of the market supplying to UK bookshops). It is likely that you will need to open a trade account with one, or both, of these wholesalers to have any hope of supplying the UK market (check to see if your SELF-PUBLISHING SERVICES PROVIDER or printer already supplies them if they are handling your distribution for you). If you want to sell to Waterstone's, you will need to open a special account with Gardners before you can approach Waterstone's to look at your book.

Gardners and Bertram Books both have websites which contain information for publishers, and this information will tell you what you need to do to open an account. They are both happy to supply self-published books—but are unlikely to physically stock the titles in quantity until demand has been proven. This does not mean that bookshops cannot get hold of your title, it just means that it is a SPECIAL ORDER item rather than an in-stock item.

There are also other wholesalers in the UK—some more specialist. And you may find that you need to open accounts with a variety of suppliers to ensure your book is as widely available as possible. Remember that if you only have one title, you are not in a very strong negotiating position when dealing with the wholesalers. They will ask for a discount on the cover price (to make it worth their while handling your book), and you will have little room to negotiate if you want your book to be available easily via the books trade. EASONS is the largest wholesaler supplying Ireland. See also LIBRARY SUPPLIERS.

WHOLESALER CATALOGUES

Each of the main wholesalers produces a variety of catalogues and magazines, which are sent to their bookshop customers, giving details of forthcoming books. The deadline to get books or adverts included in the catalogues/magazines is usually about six months in advance of the PUBLICATION DATE (as this is when most of the wholesalers' customers, the bookshops, are selecting their next stock ranges). It's possible to take adverts within the catalogues (MEDIA PACKS for them can usually be found on the wholesaler's websites).

Index

Marketing and Publicising Books
A Seriously Useful Author's Guide

This is an invaluable resource for all self-publishing authors seeking help with marketing and publicity.

A *Seriously Useful Author's Guide to Marketing and Publicising Books* aims to demystify the marketing and publicity process in a concise, lively, and highly readable way. Although primarily concerned with making sales, it also offers some very useful pre-publication advice, including the options and benefits of self-publishing. In addition it reveals some essential inside information on how the books trade works, allowing you to get an excellent understanding of your book's journey from manuscript, to publisher, to wholesaler, to retailer, to reader.

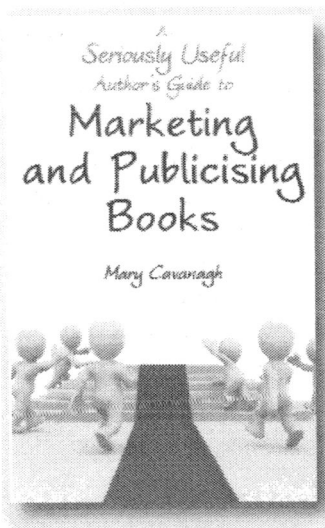

> **"A *Seriously Useful Author's Guide* simply has to be the most detailed, informative, and insightful guide to self-publicity on the market."**
> **Caro Fraser, *author***

> **"This book is an invaluable resource of information for all authors, even those who are, as yet, unpublished and contemplating the future of a fiction or non-fiction work."**
> **Deborah Lawrenson, *author***

Published April 2009   £7.99PB
ISBN 978-1848761-513   Troubador Publishing Ltd